بسم الله الرحمن الرحيم

الله

The Kingdom of the Heart

بسم الله الرحمن الرحيم

Author’s Supplication for the Translation

الفاتحة أن الله يبارك البركة الواسعة التامة الكاملة في ترجمة هذا الكتاب (مملكة القلب والأعضاء) إلى اللغة الإنجليزية وفي طباعته وفي نشره وينفع به كل من ترجم وكل من ساهم في الترجمة وكل من طبع وكل من ساهم في الطبع وكل من نشر وكل من ساهم في النشر وكل من قرأ وكل من اطلع ومن استمع وكل من سمع نفعاً عظيماً كبيراً واسعاً في الدين والدنيا والبرزخ والأخرة. واصلح لنا وللأمة شؤون الباطنة والظاهرة ويقينا وإياهم الأسوأ ويحيي قلوبنا بأنوار معرفته وأرواحنا بأنوار محبته وأسرارنا بأنوار مشاهدته وينقينا عن الشوائب ويرفعنا عليّ المراتب ويسقينا من أحلى المشارب ويصلح لنا وللأمة كل الشؤون كلها ويجعلنا مفاتيح للخير مغاليق للشر ويقبل منهم ويَسُر بذلك قلب نبيه محمد صلى الله عليه وسلم ويجعل لهم فيه الرضى الأكبر سبحانه وتعالى ويصلح الشؤون لنا ولهم في الظهور والبطون وأن يثبتنا في من ﴿يَهْدُونَ بِالْحَقِّ وَبِهِۦ يَعْدِلُونَ﴾ وإلى حضرة النبي محمد صلى الله عليه وسلم

We recite the Fātiḥa [with the intention that] Allah places vast, perfect, and complete blessings in the translation of *The Kingdom of the Heart* to English, as well as its printing and publication. May it be a source of benefit for all who translated and all who participated in its translation, for all who printed it and took part in its printing, all who published it and took part in its publication. For all who read, peruse, listen to, or hear it—may it be a source of immense, great, and wide-reaching benefit in their religion, in the life of this world, in the intermediary realm (*barzakh*), and in the hereafter. May Allah rectify our affairs, and those of the Ummah, inwardly and outwardly, and protect us and the Ummah from evil. May Allah bring life to our hearts with the lights of knowing Him, our souls with the lights of loving Him, and our inner-secrets with the lights of witnessing Him. May He purify us from all imperfections, raise us to the highest degrees, allow us to drink from the sweetest spring. May He rectify all our affairs and the affairs of the Ummah, and may He make us those who open the doors of goodness and close the doors of evil. May Allah accept this work from them, may it bring joy to the Prophet’s heart ﷺ, and may it be a means to attain His absolute pleasure ﷻ. May He rectify our affairs and theirs outwardly and inwardly and make us steadfast with those who “**who guide with the truth and establish justice accordingly**.” [Quran 7:159] May Allah grant the reward of this to the Honorable Prophet ﷺ—al-Fātiḥa.

The Kingdom of the Heart

AL-ḤABĪB
ʿUMAR BIN ḤAFĪẒ

AL-MAQASID

Published by Al-Maqasid, 2024/1445
Translated by Amjad Tarsin
Edited by Amin Buxton
Cover Design & Typesetting by
ARM (www.whitethreadpress.com)

ISBN: 978-1-7353767-1-4

CONTENTS

INTRODUCTION

All praise belongs to Allah, Lord of the Worlds, and may Allah's peace and blessings be upon His servant, the Chosen One, the Trustworthy, our master Muhammad, and upon his Family, Companions, and all those who follow his guidance until the Day of Judgment.

The distinction of the Adamic soul and uniqueness given to the human being are realized and attained through truly orienting the heart towards Allah and by following a principled methodology that guides the limbs in their actions. Allah ﷻ has decreed in His wisdom that goodness and man's true ennoblement are brought about by the uprightness of his heart and limbs. Conversely, harm, abasement, and various evils occur in the absence of that uprightness.

The following Quranic verses illustrate this point, **"And if only the townspeople had believed and been mindful of Allah, We would have showered them with blessings from the heavens and earth, but they rejected the truth and so We punished them for their misdeeds."** [Quran 7:96]

And, **"If they had been steadfast upon the right way, We would have given them abundant water to drink."** [Quran 72:16]

And, **"Had they upheld the Torah and the Gospel and what was sent down to them from their Lord, they would have been given abundance from above and from below."** [Quran 5:66]

Allah ﷻ also says, **"Corruption has manifest on land and sea as a result of people's actions and He will make them taste the conse-**

quences of some of their own actions so that they may turn back." [Quran 30:41]

And, **"Whatever misfortune befalls you, it is because of what your own hands have done—and Allah forgives much."** [Quran 42:30]

When Allah ﷻ placed our father Adam on Earth, He addressed all his progeny until the end of time as follows, **"When guidance comes to you from Me, whoever follows My guidance will neither go astray nor fall into damnation. But whoever turns away from My Reminder will certainly have a miserable life, then We will raise them up blind on the Day of Judgment."** [Quran 20:123–124]

Muslims today are in dire need of discovering the immense impacts of rectifying their heart and actions. They must remove the veils of heedlessness, neglect, and carelessness, for these are the causes of great calamities. Unfortunately, many Muslims are blind to this.

We recorded a series of lessons on this topic titled, *The Kingdom of the Heart and Limbs.*[1] A virtuous sister then transcribed the audio lessons. May Allah reward her effort and accept her endeavor. 'Abd-Allah bin 'Alī Bin Khamīs, a man of virtue who has been given Allah's enabling grace, gave his attention to the work and provided the Hadith references. Ḥusayn bin 'Awaḍ Bā Khamīs—a man of dedication, praiseworthy and blessed aims, who has acquired a good portion of sacred and beneficial knowledge—assisted in editing the work. May Allah ﷻ reward them with the best reward. And may Allah bless them in the endeavor they took on and make them sources of goodness and benefit for the Ummah of the Prophet Muhammad, may Allah's peace and blessings be upon him, his Family, and his Companions.

May Allah make all their efforts purely for the sake of His Noble Countenance and decree great benefit through them. Enabling grace

1 This series was broadcast in the most blessed month of Ramadan.

(*tawfiq*) is through Allah, all trust is placed in Him, and there is neither power nor ability save by Him. May Allah's peace and blessings be upon our master Muhammad and upon his Family and Companions. All praise belongs to Allah, the Lord of the Worlds.

ʿHABIBʾ ʿUMAR BIN MUHAMMAD BIN SĀLIM
BIN ḤAFĪẒ IBN AL-SHAYKH ABŪ BAKR BIN SĀLIM

CHAPTER 1

The Connection Between the Heart & Limbs

All praise belongs to Allah, the Sovereign, the Real, the Apparent. He gives from His dominion what He wills, and Allah is Vast and All-Knowing. I bear witness there is no god except Allah, One without partner, who revealed to His Chosen Servant, **"Say, 'O Allah! Lord over all authorities! You give authority to whomever You please and remove it from whom You please; You honor whomever You please and disgrace whom You please—all good is in Your Hands. Surely You are Most Capable of everything.'"** [Quran 3:26]

I bear witness that our master, Prophet, guide, and leader, Muhammad, is His Servant and Messenger, entrusted with His revelation. He conveyed on behalf of Allah ﷻ what he was commanded to convey to creation in the best and most perfect way. The hearts of those who were granted nobility by the Creator ﷻ in pre-eternity responded to the call and followed his way of guidance.

To proceed: Allah ﷻ has placed unique qualities within the human being that make him distinct. Within every human being is a Kingdom. The heart is the ruler of this Kingdom, and the rest of the body are its subjects. If the heart rules with justice and excellence, the body will perform good actions and the Kingdom will flourish.

If, however, the heart neglects its duties or is unjust, the body will be in a state of disobedience to Allah ﷻ and the entire Kingdom will suffer the consequences. Allah made this Kingdom so crucial that through it the eternal and everlasting dominion of the next life is either gained or lost.

Magnificent indeed is this Kingdom, which, if ruled justly, will allow a person to enter the limitless dominion of the Hereafter. Allah ﷻ says about this, **"And if you could see it, you would behold bliss and a great kingdom."** [Quran 76:20] Conversely, if a person misrules their Kingdom, it can cause them to miss out on that vast dominion, and what a terrible loss that would be.

THE DISTINCTION OF THE HUMAN HEART

By virtue of the uniqueness of the human heart, which was given to us by Allah ﷻ, the limbs have acquired an immense rank and significance. We should therefore reflect on and understand that the heart is the basis for one's actions, regardless of the time, place, or situation one is in. Allah's main concern is with what takes place in the hearts of His servants, as the Prophet ﷺ said, *"Allah does not look at your bodies or your outward forms, but rather He looks at your hearts and actions."*[2]

Allah has made everything in existence glorify Him, but He has given a special kind of knowledge of Him only to those who possess the intellect: mankind, jinn, and angels. The distinction given to the human being lies in his ability to know Allah, the Most Merciful, the Creator, the Originator, the Initiator, the Resurrector, the Possessor of the beginning and the One to Whom belongs the return ﷻ. One only attains this distinction, which is direct knowledge of Allah (*ma'rifa*), through his heart and not any other part of his body. The heart is what makes the human being unique—it is his source of honor, the means for his salvation, and through it he attains the Greater Kingdom of Paradise.

2 Narrated by Muslim (2564).

THE CONNECTION BETWEEN THE HEART AND LIMBS

We should be aware of the relationship between physical actions and the heart. What differentiates the actions of believers and disbelievers, the righteous and corrupt is their hearts. Actions are considered good or evil based on the state of the heart.

After acknowledging this, we delve into understanding the soul. Being ignorant of the soul prevents one from knowing Allah سبحانه وتعالى as illustrated in the following verses, **"Do not be like those who forgot Allah, so He made them forget their own souls. It is they who are ˹truly˺ rebellious. Not equal are the residents of the Fire and the residents of Paradise—the residents of Paradise are the successful ones."** [Quran 59:19–20] These verses indicate that the residents of Paradise are those who remembered Allah سبحانه وتعالى and forgot neither Him nor their own souls. They regulated their actions for the time that they were in this world, motivated to do so by their belief in Allah سبحانه وتعالى. Their hearts were aware of the purpose and wisdom of their existence, and their special rank in this world. All of this is necessary for anyone preparing for the journey to the Hereafter. It is the means to attain felicity, assistance from the Sovereign Lord, eternal bliss, and a vast Kingdom.

Everything is based on the connection between the heart and limbs. This is why all physical acts of worship have a purpose connected to the heart. All acts of obedience are dependent upon one's intentions and motivations, which take place in the heart. Belief in Allah سبحانه وتعالى and His Messengers عليهم السلام is foundational in guiding a person's actions. This belief impacts the choices a person makes and shapes what pleases and displeases him.

Unfortunately, heedlessness is widespread among many people of faith, preventing them from giving their faith its proper due. They assume that faith is merely lip service or belief in the basic tenets such as the existence of Allah سبحانه وتعالى, His Decree, His complete knowledge of

His creation, and that the ultimate return is to Him. But they do not give belief its proper place in their hearts, and thus it does not steer their every word and action.

This heedlessness has caused many believers to imitate non-believers. We have been given ritual acts of worship and sacred seasons to help us overcome heedlessness. They include the month of Ramadan, the Hajj season, the new Islamic year, the sacred months, the commemoration of the Prophet Muhammad's birth ﷺ, his Prophethood, migration, battles, and his Night Journey and Heavenly Ascension (*Isrā' wā Mi'rāj*). Commemorating these occasions strengthens the connection between the limbs and true faith within the heart, which then dispels the darkness of heedlessness. Being heedless has led people to consider these sacred seasons and their acts of worship as insignificant; has prevented them from celebrating and understanding the wisdom of these occasions; and has weakened their faith, which assists in governing their actions.

Therefore, the believer needs to understand completely that Allah's gaze is upon his heart. The actions of our limbs are only judged according to what is established in our hearts.

THE REALITY AND ROLE OF THE HEART

You are only human by virtue of your heart and soul, not merely by way of your body. After understanding this, you come to know that your distinction is only attained through disciplining and purifying your lower self (*nafs*) and through recognizing the purpose of the heart which you have been given. By the 'heart' we do not mean the organ referred to in medicine and anatomy. Rather, by the 'heart' we mean the sublime spiritual entity which is part of the divine command. It is the divinely bestowed subtle faculty that Allah has addressed, through which one receives reward or punishment, good or evil, and judgment or reckoning. This subtle faculty that Allah ﷻ has given to every human is the place of moral accountability (*taklīf*). Anyone lacking this faculty and the power of reasoning is not accountable before Allah.

The heart's purpose is not merely to give you the same consciousness as animals. An animal's consciousness helps it distinguish between what benefits or harms its physical body, as well as other immediate benefits related to its temporal livelihood. This level of consciousness is shared with animals, even insects, all by the command of Allah ﷻ. The human being's consciousness is greater.

Although the wonders found within the ant or bee kingdoms provide profound guidance with regards to the amazing capabilities that Allah gives creation, the distinction He granted you is much greater. You have the capability to distinguish between what brings eternal reward and what brings never-ending punishment. In reality, your distinction is in knowing the greatness of Allah, Who created you and everything that surrounds you.

You are the possessor of an exalted Kingdom by virtue of your heart, and your other body parts are at its command. This is Allah's wondrous decree which He has placed within man's nature. Therefore, it is only fitting that you come to know your heart, its distinctiveness, its unique purpose, and to comprehend that its state will determine the outcome of the all-important final return. By knowing the heart, you come to know yourself and your Lord ﷻ. You then will be able to prepare to welcome the seasons of worship (such as the blessed month of Ramadan) with excellence, treating them in a way befitting of one who realizes that he has a Creator and that he must prepare for the meeting with Him.

May Allah ﷻ make us as such, and may He prepare us for an excellent return to and most noble meeting with Him. May we meet Him in the best of states, the states of those whom He is pleased and content with. May Allah's peace and blessings be upon our master Muhammad and his Family and Companions. All praise belongs to Allah, Lord of the Worlds.

CHAPTER 2

Actions are based on the Heart

All praise belongs to Allah, Who extends His grace to every seeker who turns to Him. We bear witness that He is Allah. There is no god besides Him, and He has no partner. We bear witness that our master, Prophet, and the coolness of our eyes, Muhammad, is His Servant and Messenger, and the guide who leads people to Him. May Allah's peace be upon him, his Family, Companions, and all who adopt his etiquettes and follow his path until the end of time.

To proceed: Each person's mission in this life, which is the abode of accountability (*taklīf*), is to fulfill the Trust[3] that even the heavens and the earth were unable to bear. This Trust is a great honor granted by Allah ﷻ. The one who bears it has a higher rank than the heavens and the earth and everything in them. Allah ﷻ says, **"Indeed, We offered the trust to the heavens and the earth and the mountains, but they ⌜all⌝ declined to bear it, being fearful of it. But mankind assumed it. Truly he is inept and foolish."** [Quran 33:72]

If a person fails to give this Trust its due and is heedless of the distinction and status granted to him by his Lord, he has chosen to abase his own soul by disobeying its Creator ﷻ. As a result, this person falls to a

3 This Trust pertains to belief in Allah ﷻ and fulfilling His commandments.

status lower than that of cattle and other animals. Allah ﷾ says regarding those who are heedless of this reality, **"Indeed, We have destined many jinn and humans for Hell. They have hearts they do not understand with, eyes they do not see with, and ears they do not hear with. They are like cattle; in fact, they are even less guided! These are the utterly heedless."** [Quran 7:179] Observe the connection between the heart, seeing, and hearing in the Quranic verse, **"They have hearts they do not understand with, eyes they do not see with, and ears they do not hear with. . ."** This is the secret of the link between the heart and limbs, which was discussed in the previous chapter.

Allah's connecting hearing and seeing to the heart implies that one must be mindful of the risks associated with these two senses. Allah ﷾ combined the three and said, **"Hearing, sight, and heart—you will be questioned about all of these."** [Quran 17:36] Since hearing and sight are senses that help one understand and perceive, they are the two doors to the heart. Whatever reaches the heart through them has a powerful effect on it.

A believer who grasps the secret of the connection between his heart and limbs must never be neglectful of rectifying his heart and thereby regulating the actions of his limbs. By doing so, he ensures that his actions do not become a source of remorse on the Day of Resurrection—and how dreadful will remorse be on that Day! Allah ﷾ says, **"The record of deeds will be laid open and you will see the wicked in fear of what is ⌜written⌝ in it. They will cry, 'Woe to us! What kind of record is this that does not leave any sin, large or small, unaccounted for?' They will find everything they ever did laid before them."** [Quran 18:49]

RECTIFYING ONE'S ACTIONS

You have the ability to move, observe, listen, walk, take, withhold, and make different choices. You live within the sphere of accountability;

therefore, rectify your heart in a way that improves your actions. Otherwise, you expose yourself to regret and remorse. **"And warn them ⌜O Prophet⌝ of the Day of Regret, when all matters will be settled, while they are ⌜engrossed⌝ in heedlessness and disbelief."** [Quran 19:39]

This rectification calls for a thorough study of the forces that Allah ﷻ has designated for the heart. Among these forces are anger and desire, two forces that Allah has placed within human beings. The wisdom of this is to distinguish between two groups: those who use them in beneficial ways that guarantee felicity; and those who use them according to their whims, not differentiating between the consequences of one action or another.

You are an intelligent person; therefore, you must realize that Allah ﷻ has placed anger as a force within you so that you may strive to fulfill your duties. This is done by controlling your anger and making it abide by the dictates of the intellect and the Sacred Law, being angered only when Allah requires you to be, so that your anger is only stirred for the sake of Allah. We learn this from the life of our Prophet Muhammad ﷺ, whose anger and contentment were only for the sake of Allah ﷻ.

When someone sees a wrong being done, this arouses a type of righteous anger. This anger produces courage, causing one to challenge the wrong that has been done. They then defend Islam and their own or other people's lives, dignity, and property. Anger is also used to purify the greed of the lower self and balance one's desires so that they do not cause one to transgress. When anger is regulated and balanced, it produces righteous qualities within a person. Such a person becomes well-mannered and diligent.

If anger is imbalanced, whether on the side of absence or of excess, it produces negative qualities that jeopardize one's dignity and exalted status. Excessive anger makes him reckless or harmful, like a predatory animal who is ready to show aggression to anyone who disagrees with his whims or wishes. This causes chaos and turmoil in society. On the other hand, the absence of anger results in cowardice and feeblemindedness. It opens the door to attacks by enemies and wrongdoing by oppressors. It even causes people to abandon their values and principles. Therefore, anger is necessary, but it must be balanced.

CONNECTING OUTWARD ACTIONS TO THE HEART

The rectification of one's character traits can be achieved in several ways. One is through the various obligatory acts of worship, such as fasting Ramadan. When the act of fasting emanates from a believing heart, it refines a person's soul. When Allah ﷻ mentions fasting in the Quran, He begins by addressing people of faith, **"O believers! Fasting is prescribed for you—as it was for those before you—so that perhaps you will become mindful ⌜of Allah⌝."** [Quran 2:183] Fasting must be motivated by faith to have an impact on one's soul. When this is the case, it results in consistently being mindful of Allah (*taqwā*), which then governs one's anger and desire. In a Hadith Qudsi, Allah ﷻ mentions how fasting is meant to regulate desires, ***"He abstains from his food, drink, and desire for My sake."***[4]

Another way to rectify one's character traits is through the Prayer. Allah ﷻ tells us that, **"Prayer deters from indecency and wickedness."** [Quran 29:45] The Prayer contains nothing obvious that keeps us from indecency and wickedness. However, when the motivation for the Prayer comes from a heart that believes in the One to Whom we pray, it yields the fruit of vigilance and rectifies the mechanism for vigilance within the heart. This motivation also creates a yearning for Allah that causes one to hate any form of indecency, wickedness, and forbidden actions that would distance him from Allah ﷻ.

This brings us to a realization that is often overlooked: that our physical acts of worship are related to the conditions of our hearts. The

4 Narrated by Aḥmad and Ibn Abī Shayba.

supreme concern is the heart. What matters is not mere bodily actions (even if a person goes so far as to sacrifice his own life); rather, the concern is what is firmly established in the heart.

Thus, rectifying outward actions must be based on a sound connection to the heart. The motivation from the heart must be true and founded on sincerity. We read in the Hadith, *"Whoever fasts Ramadan faithfully and in anticipation ⌜of reward⌝ shall be forgiven his previous sins."*[5] And, *"Whoever stands ⌜in worship⌝ in Ramadan faithfully and in anticipation ⌜of reward⌝ shall be forgiven his previous sins."*[6] This shows us what a remarkable teacher the Messenger of Allah ﷺ was. Allah ﷻ entrusted him with the purification of humanity, as mentioned in the Noble Quran, **"It is He Who has sent the illiterate people a Messenger from among themselves, reciting to them His Revelations and purifying them. . ."** [Quran 62:2]

He says ﷺ, *". . .faithfully and in anticipation ⌜of reward⌝"* in order to connect us to the proper motivation we must have when fasting, when standing in prayer, and in all other righteous actions.

Most Muslims do not see the connection between the actions of the body and the state of the heart. We must be mindful of this point. We must also be aware that actions that emanate from a faithful heart have great esteem in the sight of the One Whom we worship and serve, Allah ﷻ.

May Allah ﷻ make us steadfast in sincerely seeking His Noble Countenance and in being true with Him. May He adorn our bodily actions with lights that emanate from hearts that are pure and true. May Allah's peace and blessings be upon His Prophet, the Chosen One, our master Muhammad, and upon his Family and Companions. All praise belongs to Allah, Lord of the Worlds.

---

5 Narrated by al-Bukhārī in *Kitāb al-Īmān* (Hadith 38), and Muslim in *Kitāb Ṣalāh al-Musāfirīn wa Qasrihā* (Hadith 760).

6 Narrated by al-Bukhārī in *Kitāb al-Tarāwīḥ* (Hadith 1904), and Muslim in *Kitāb Ṣalāh al-Musāfirīn* (Hadith 759).

CHAPTER 3

The Tongue and Its Effects

All praise belongs to Allah, the Turner of Hearts. He is the One Who makes the hearts of whomever He wills steadfast upon what He loves. **"Allah makes the believers steadfast with the firm Word ˹of faith˺ in this worldly life and the Hereafter, but Allah leaves the wrongdoers to stray. For Allah does whatever He wills."** [Quran 14:27] We bear witness that there is no god but Allah, One without partner. And we bear witness that our master Muhammad is His Servant and Messenger. He informed us that, *"Truly, within the body there is a piece of flesh, if it is sound, the entire body is sound. But if it is corrupted, the entire body is corrupted. It is the heart."*[7] O Allah, send peace and blessings upon our master Muhammad—through whom You brought the believers' hearts to life—and upon his Family, Companions, and all who keep to his path until the Day of Judgment.

To proceed: Allah ﷻ has made it such that when one speaks, the motivation to do so stems from the heart. Subsequently, the words uttered then have an impact on the heart. This occurs with both acts of obedience and disobedience. Physical actions begin as a motivation in the heart, and after the heart motivates the limbs to act, the effect of that action returns

7 Narrated by al-Bukhārī in *Kitāb al-Īmān* (Hadith 152), and Muslim in *Kitāb al-Musāqāh* (Hadith 1599).

to the heart. If a believer performs an act of obedience (such as recitation of the Quran, Prayer, charity, fasting, Hajj, ʿUmrah, or maintaining ties of kinship) with sincerity, his motivation is pleasing to Allah ﷻ. When he performs that act of obedience, a light emanates from the action that returns to the heart, thus increasing it in light.

Conversely, the motivation for all sin also originates from the heart, beginning with a thought that passes through it. If the heart is not regulated by vigilance (*murāqaba*) and lacks conviction in the Prophet's message ﷺ, then the evil thought resonates with it, and the thought turns into a resolve to act. The person then performs the sin, which produces a darkness that returns to the heart, increasing its darkness. This is what is meant by the narration, "Whoever commits a sin, a portion of the intellect departs and never returns to him again."[8] This is because the best he can do in this case is to follow up the bad deed with a good deed that erases it; but if the good deed had come about without a bad deed occurring before it, the heart would have increased in brightness from the very beginning! However, when it was preceded by a bad deed, the heart did not increase in brightness. The most that the good deed could do was to purify the heart from the effect of the sin. This detracts from a person and irreversibly impairs his intellect.

WORSHIP'S IMPACT ON RECTIFYING ONE'S SPEECH

A person's words have a strong connection to what is in the heart. Once spoken, those words impact the heart. Acts of worship play a strong role in regulating one's speech. For example, speaking to any created being invalidates the Prayer. The only exception is for Allah's Messenger ﷺ, for he is addressed with the greetings of *salām* in the Prayer, and it is only valid for the one praying to say: "Peace be upon you, O Prophet, and the

8 Imam al-Ghazālī quotes this in the *Iḥyā'* and al-ʿIrāqī said that he could not find its source.

mercy of Allah and His blessings" [*As-salāmu ʿalayka ayyuha'l Nabīyyu wa raḥmatullāhi wa barakātuh*]. The Companions would say, "He ﷺ would teach us the *tashhahud* just as he would teach us a Sūra from the Quran."[9] In all of the narrations of the *tashhahud,* it states, *"Peace be upon you, O Prophet, and the mercy of Allah and His blessings."*[10] We are prohibited from speaking in the Prayer to any other created being in existence. The Prophet ﷺ said, *"It is improper to speak to people during the Prayer."*[11] Prayer thus regulates our speech.

With respect to fasting, the Prophet ﷺ said, *"If someone does not leave false testimony and acting upon it, then Allah has no need for him to leave his food and drink."*[12] He explained that if fasting is not based on a firm foundation of *taqwā* stemming from the heart, then it does not inhibit the one fasting from false testimony (which is any statement that contradicts the truth or is prohibited by the Sacred Law). Another Hadith states, *"Fasting is a shield, so on a day when one of you is fasting, do not yell nor say obscene or vile words. If someone insults him or affronts him, he should say, 'I am fasting.'"*[13]

You now understand that a person who has no care for what he utters risks losing all the treasures and spiritual experiences that worship yields—leaving him with only the empty *form* of worship, which does not benefit him. Considering even the pinnacle of righteous actions, which is struggling in the way of Allah ﷻ (*jihād*), when someone said of a person who was killed in battle, "Good tidings of Paradise for him!" the Messenger of Allah ﷺ asked him, *"How do you know that? Maybe he used to speak about what did not concern him and was tightfisted with wealth*

9 Narrated by Muslim in his *Ṣaḥīḥ* on the authority of Ibn ʿAbbās in *Kitāb al-Ṣalāh* (Hadith 403).

10 Translator's Note: Saying, *Assalāmu ʿalayka ayyuha al-Nabīyyu wa raḥmatullāhi wa barakātuh.*

11 Narrated by Muslim in *Kitāb al-Ṣalāh* (Hadith 537).

12 Narrated by al-Bukhārī in *Kitāb al-Masājid wa Mawāḍiʿ al-Ṣalāh* (Hadith 1804), and by al-Nasāʾī and al-Bayhaqī.

13 Narrated by Aḥmad on the authority of Abū Hurayra.

that he did not need."[14] Maybe he had the disease of speaking without restraint or vigilance. This is a calamity, yet many are afflicted with it!

A child may hear a foul word from his or her parents that then becomes embedded within that child's heart and remains there. The child then utters that word many times in his or her life. That neglectful parent, who had not realized that a human being's most precious possession is his heart, carries that burden. The trust—the heart of this child—is placed on the shoulders of that child's mother and father. These parents were oblivious to this and betrayed the trust placed in the hearts of their children. They said or did bad things in front of their children, corrupting their hearts. This corruption might linger with that child for the rest of his or her life—and we seek refuge in Allah ﷾.

Therefore, we must be mindful of what we say (and allow others to say) to our children and families, wherever we may be. We find this command mentioned explicitly by Allah in the Quran, **"Tell My servants to say only what is best."** [Quran 17:53] He also says ﷾, **"And speak to all people with goodness."** [Quran 2:83] He commanded us to speak to people *with* goodness. **"*With* goodness"**—ponder this! Allah uses the verbal noun. He did not say, 'say what is good.' In other words, choose words that embody the reality of beauty and goodness.[15] Say these words such that your speech is intrinsically good, not merely an act of goodness. In the other verse, He ﷾ says, **"Tell My ⌜believing⌝ servants to say only what is best."** [Quran 17:53] Therefore, when you have two words in mind that are both good, choose the better of two.

14 Narrated by al-Bayhaqī in *Shuʿab al-Īmān.*

15 Translator's Note: Imam Fakhr al-Dīn al-Rāzī says in his *Tafsīr*, commenting on this verse and specifically the word *ḥusnā* (goodness), "This means a statement that is intrinsically good due to its extensive goodness."

RECTIFYING YOUR SPEECH IS PART OF FAITH

Many believers are heedless of these remarkable directives, and this is only due to their failure to conform to the dictates of faith. This divide between the limbs and heart has created a divide between man and his Creator, separating him from truly attaining nearness to Him. This Hadith highlights the relationship between the two, *"Whoever believes in Allah and the Last Day, then let him say what is good or keep silent."*[16]

Since when were you allowed to think lightly of the tremendousness of the One who gave you the ability to be silent? You choose to say whatever you want and freely disobey Him and go against His command.

"And speak to all people with goodness" [Quran 2:83]—make your speech the embodiment of beauty, have people's hearts and souls love your words, and bring joy to whoever hears them.

Let us then take this lesson from the Prayer and from fasting: we must rectify our speech and avoid words that we have been cautioned against. This is so crucial that the Prophet ﷺ said, *"A man may say a word that earns him Allah's wrath, but he thinks nothing of it; yet due to it, he plummets into Hellfire."*[17] Another narration states, *"A man may say a word that he sees as harmless, yet due to it he plummets for seventy years in the Fire."*[18]

We must then, in fulfilling the covenant with Allah ﷻ, be fully aware of our speech. We must adorn our fasting with beautiful speech and by avoiding evil words. Lying, backbiting, talebearing, and false testimony are some of the things that detract from a person's reward for fasting. *"If someone does not leave aside false testimony and acting upon it, then Allah has no need for him to leave his food and drink."*[19] Let us learn the lessons taken from the various acts of worship that relate to regulating our speech.

16 Narrated by al-Bukhārī in *Kitāb al-Adab* (Hadith 5672), and by Muslim in *Kitāb al-Īmān* (Hadith 47).

17 Narrated by al-Bukhārī in *Kitāb al-Riqāq* (Hadith 6113).

18 Narrated by al-Tirmidhī in *Abwāb al-Zuhd ʿan Rasūl Illāh* ﷺ (Hadith 2416).

19 Narrated by al-Bukhārī in *Kitāb al-Ṣawm* (Hadith 1903) and al-Tirmidhī in *Abwāb*

THE EFFECT OF THE TONGUE'S UPRIGHTNESS ON THE LIMBS

The Prophet ﷺ informed us that the limbs plead with the tongue every day, saying, *"Be mindful of Allah with regard to us. We are dependent on you: if you are upright, we will be upright; and if you deviate, we will deviate."*[20] Here we see the immense effect speech has on the rest of the body.

When Allah ﷻ said, **"Tell My servants to say only what is best. . .,"** He mentioned that one of the reasons for this is that **". . .the devil certainly seeks to sow discord among them."** [Quran 17:53] This means that when people do not say what is best, the Devil then seizes the opportunity to sow discord. People give the Devil a chance to come between them by being careless with their words. This is further emphasized by the Hadith of Prophet ﷺ, *"A good word is charity."*[21] We must deliver this charity to those we converse with and be mindful of the virtue of excellent speech.

We turn to our Lord ﷻ and ask Him to grant us such faith that gives us the strength to regulate our tongues. One of the knowers of Allah (*ʿārifīn*) said, "Whenever I see a person have piety (*taqwā*) in his speech, I see it affect all his states and affairs."

O Allah, rectify our tongues, allow us to use them in Your remembrance and in saying that which benefits people. Protect us from words that lead to painful and unbearable punishment—O Sovereign, O Creator, O Lord of the Worlds! May Allah's peace and blessings be upon the Chosen One, Muhammad, and upon his Family and Companions. All praise belongs to Allah, Lord of the Worlds.

al-Ṣawm (Hadith 707).

20 Narrated by al-Tirmidhī (Hadith 2518).

21 Narrated by al-Bukhārī (Hadith 2827) and Muslim (Hadith 1009).

CHAPTER 4

The Tongue's Role in Cultivating the Individual & Society

All praise belongs to Allah, the Sovereign, the Real, the Evident. We bear witness that He is Allah. There is no god except Him, One without partner. His Words are the truth and to Him belongs the dominion on the Day when the Trumpet is blown. We bear witness that Muhammad, our master and Prophet, is His Servant and Messenger. He was sent by Allah ﷻ with the truth and clear light. O Allah, send your peace, mercy, and blessings upon him, his Family, Companions, and whoever follows his path until the Day of Judgment.

To proceed: This exalted Kingdom given to the human being in the form of the heart and body—and all it contains of great secrets by which compensation and settlement in either Paradise or the Fire are decided—deserves extensive consideration and examination. We mentioned previously the relationship between speech and the heart, and that the tongue's uprightness affects all the limbs, and that its effect returns to the heart.

This is why people of spiritual cultivation (*tarbīya*) are careful to ensure that their children become accustomed to saying '*Bismillāh*' [In the Name of Allah] as soon as they are able to speak. They constantly repeat the Name of the Real ﷻ, the Name of Majesty: *Allāh*—hoping that their children's tongues become beautified through mentioning Allah's Name as soon as they begin to speak, and that their speech begins with the light of connectedness to Allah, the Creator ﷻ.

THE TONGUE'S IMPACT ON PEOPLE'S RELATIONSHIP WITH SOCIETY

The tongue has an immense impact on both the individual and his surroundings, which is one of the reasons why the Quran commands us to say what is best. When this is implemented by families, they are much more likely to maintain harmony and avoid discord and the breaking of family ties. They must choose their words carefully and accustom themselves to saying what is most beautiful. Families need to cultivate these virtues within children and teach them to avoid listening to bad words. This is foundational to their upbringing and development and comes before cautioning them against saying bad words.

Teaching children to avoid listening to idle speech and bad words is a basic religious principle. The Quran teaches us to turn away from those who ridicule the verses of Allah ﷻ, **"And when you come across those who ridicule Our revelations, turn away from them until they move on to another topic."** [Quran 6:68] Allah ﷻ also says, **"Then do not sit in that company unless they engage in a different topic, or else you will be like them."** [Quran 4:140]

We now know that listening to bad words—whether it be directly or through some type of media—has a substantial effect on the one hearing them. Many Muslims have disregarded the foundations of raising their children in a way that will enable them to truly establish the Kingdom of the Heart. Those who successfully establish it will receive glad tidings in the life of this world and the next. This shows that the tongue's affair is immense.

Likewise, listening to an obscene word has an effect on the heart that can be difficult to remove, which is why the Imams of Islam would strive to carefully protect youth and children from listening to bad words. Some even taught their children not to go to public places where they were likely to hear such words.

We only mention these things to encourage people to understand the obligations and responsibilities related to core principles. In fact, this topic relates to the cultivation and elevation of the human soul itself. Many people's hearts and minds have become neglectful of this important issue despite the explicit Quranic and Prophetic commands related to it. Let us take steps to address this great disparity between the level of careful cultivation of children and the decline that has occurred within the Ummah—which has reached such a point that people even hear obscene words from young children!

This decline is caused by the fact that heedlessness dominates the hearts of many Muslims. They are careless of the evil words they utter, those that their sons or daughters listen to (which harden their hearts and fill them with darkness), and such words that impede their ability and that of their children to heed Allah's Words ﷻ with excellence.

ENVISIONING THE RECKONING WHEN SPEAKING

Each Muslim must be conscious of the fact that Allah ﷻ will directly address them on the Day of Resurrection regarding the tongue and the words that emanate from it. However, someone who excessively uses bad language is not fit to be addressed by the All-Knowing King ﷻ. As Allah says regarding a certain group of people, **"Allah will neither speak to them, nor look at them, nor purify them on the Day of Resurrection—and they will suffer a painful punishment."** [Quran 3:77] Anyone who anticipates that he will address his True Lord ﷻ directly will strive to prepare his tongue to respond with excellence when Allah questions him. He will then be able to successfully address Him because he used his tongue in a way that was pleasing to Allah ﷾ and protected it from words that warrant His wrath.

If you wish to address Allah ﷾, His Prophets, Messengers, the Entirely True (*Ṣiddīqūn*), martyrs, and righteous, you must realize the great sanctity placed within your speech. You must give attention to regulating your speech and words. Whenever Abū Bakr al-Ṣiddīq رضي الله عنه, who was taught directly by the Chosen One Muhammad ﷺ, would speak, he would carry a stone with him and place it in his mouth. He did this out of fear that he would say something displeasing to his Creator or something that his Lord ﷾ would not reward him for. Do not be surprised by this, for if you knew the consequences of your words, then you would recognize that this is the proper way to act. This is the way of the people of virtue, those who understand the immensity of the Hereafter and of being addressed by the Almighty ﷾.

A person holds himself to a higher standard when he addresses officials, knowing that they will scrutinize his words. He knows that any mistake or error in an expression will have significant consequences that could lead to suspension, blame, or being reported (stating, for example, that he is part of such-and-such movement or holds certain political views). Therefore, he is concerned with and aware of the weight of each of his words. Many people in such a situation avoid impromptu speech, reading instead from a written speech that they reviewed meticulously beforehand. All of this is done to avoid being held accountable by people. But whoever realizes that the Lord of the heavens and the earth's account is far greater knows that the ideal path to follow is the one taken by the people of virtue: those who are conscientious of the words they speak and who fear that a slip of the tongue will make their feet falter.

Whoever speaks excessively about what does not concern him will make abundant errors; and whoever makes abundant errors will have plenty of sins; and whoever's sins are plenty, the Fire has more right to him. Therefore, it is necessary to choose a good word that has a positive impact on people's hearts and serves as a charity given to them.

GOOD SPEECH AND ITS FRUITS

It is necessary for children, women, and men to become accustomed to saying what is good and speaking only with goodness, as Allah سبحانه وتعالى commands us in the Quran. As people who believe in Allah, the meeting with Him, and the Reckoning, we must ensure that good words inform our thoughts and objectives. Let us remember what has been mentioned to us in the Book, when Allah سبحانه وتعالى says, **"As the two recording angels note everything, ⌜one⌝ sitting to his right and ⌜the other⌝ to his left, not a single word does he utter without having a vigilant observer ready ⌜to write it down⌝."** [Quran 50:17–18]

Our tongues are also a means for us to acquire virtues and attain exalted stations. This is achieved by reciting the Quran, reading Hadith, and by recounting the stories of the Prophets, Messengers, and the righteous. Each of these resources contain great lessons for people of understanding. Those who claim to have the solutions to life's problems (whether socially, economically, or intellectually), tell us many stories and present them to us in a variety of ways. Meanwhile in the Quran, Allah سبحانه وتعالى has selected stories about the Prophets and *Awlīyāʾ* and tells us about those who opposed them and what happened to them. What place do these divinely selected stories have in our lives, our homes, and in our conversations? What role do they play for both the young and old, for families and societies? We must give our attention to the accounts revealed by Allah سبحانه وتعالى.

Additionally, through the tongue, you can become someone who makes abundant remembrance of Allah سبحانه وتعالى. You are then someone who Allah mentions, and He is likely to forgive your wrongdoings and make you one of His elect servants. Allah سبحانه وتعالى said, **"Men and women who**

remember Allah often—for them Allah has prepared forgiveness and a great reward." [Quran 33:35]

Furthermore, guidance, which is needed in all aspects of life and helps people remain steadfast, is conveyed to people through the tongue. It is crucial for a person to know the value of his speech and to prepare himself for when his deeds will be weighed on the Scales.

O Allah, make us steadfast upon the truth in what we say, do, and believe. O Allah, bless us in what we say and in what we refrain from saying. Make us steadfast upon what You are pleased with so that You inspire us to say '*Lā ilāha illa Allāh*' at the time of passing—O Living and Self-Subsistent! May Allah send peace and blessings upon our master Muhammad, and upon his Family and Companions. All praise belongs to Allah, Lord of the Worlds.

CHAPTER 5

The Power of Hearing

All praise belongs to Allah, the Protector, the Judge. We bear witness that He is Allah. There is no god except Him, One without partner. He gathers creation on the Day when deeds are placed on the Scales. We bear witness that our master and Prophet Muhammad is His Servant and Messenger. The Quran was revealed to him, and he conveyed the message from Allah ﷻ, which is a means for everyone to attain felicity. May Allah's peace and blessings upon our master Muhammad, his Family, Companions, and all those who tread his path with excellence.

To proceed: The human being, in the Kingdom he has been given, is able to live a good life by following divine guidance and rectifying his heart, which is the place where direct knowledge of Allah (*ma'rifa*) resides. When the heart is rectified, the rest of the body will be in a state of obedience to Allah ﷻ. Whoever strives to achieve this by following the luminous lamp[22] sent as a mercy from Allah to all the Worlds ﷺ attains felicity in this life, at the time of death, and after death.

22 Translator's note: This is one of the titles Allah gives His Beloved Messenger ﷺ in the Quran, **"O Prophet! We have sent you as a witness, and a deliverer of good news, and a warner, and a caller to Allah by His command, and a luminous lamp."** [Quran 33:45–46]

THE IMPORTANCE OF HEARING

Part of this great and vast Kingdom is hearing, which is one of the signs of Allah's marvelous power and magnificent wisdom سبحانه وتعالى. He created hearing, providing the ear with thousands of receptor cells, so that meanings could reach the consciousness and be translated. The heart is then able to issue directives to the limbs based on the judgment it made from the sound that it had heard.

Just as what we say has grave consequences, so too does what we hear. What we hear plants seeds in our heart, for both good or evil. Allah سبحانه وتعالى says, **"So ˹Prophet˺ give good news to My servants—those who listen to what is said and follow the best of it."** [Quran 39:17–18] Hearing is a faculty that allows us to attain distinction and ascend in the degrees of Allah's elect servants.

The ability to hear is a gift from Allah. No one is capable of increasing or decreasing their ability to hear. If someone has poor hearing, his only option is to take the means and medical treatment in accordance with what Allah سبحانه وتعالى decrees and facilitates. So be mindful of Allah regarding your hearing and what you listen to. What do you expose your friends, children, and family to? What do you make them hear? The All-Hearing, All-Seeing سبحانه وتعالى observes what you listen to and what you have His servants listen to.

Words and voices have a powerful influence on people's convictions, perspectives, and choices. You must protect your hearing just as you would protect your tongue from dishonorable speech. When you listen to sinful words, you are like the one who spoke it. Allah سبحانه وتعالى said, **"He has already revealed to you in the Book that when you hear Allah's revelations being denied or ridiculed, then do not sit in that company unless they engage in a different topic, or else you will be like them."** [Quran 4:140] And He سبحانه وتعالى said, **". . .once you remember, do not ˹continue to˺ sit with the wrongdoing people."** [Quran 6:68] The poet said:

Protect your hearing from vile language,
Just as you would protect your tongue from uttering it
When you listen to something abominable,
You become like the one saying it, so be careful!

ENDEAVORING TO ONLY LISTEN TO GOOD

The need to fulfill our duty in our homes and elsewhere regarding what we, those in our care, and our companions listen to was previously mentioned. If you hope to hear words of contentment from Allah ﷻ when meeting Him, then you must only listen to that which pleases Him. Therefore, when someone hears slander, it is an obligation for him to refute the one uttering those evil words, to not believe him, and to reprimand him. He should not let that slander make him seek out the flaws of the person mentioned, and he must protect his heart from any negative feelings toward that person.

When a man came to ʿUmar ibn ʿAbd al-ʿAzīz maligning another person, he said to him, "Listen, if you want, we can investigate this matter. But if you are lying, then you are of the people mentioned in the verse, **'O believers, if an evildoer brings you any news, verify ⌜it⌝ so you do not harm people unknowingly, becoming regretful for what you have done.'** [Quran 49:6] And if you are speaking the truth, then you are of the people of this verse, **'Backbiter, tale-bearer, withholder of good, transgressor, evildoer, coarse, and—on top of all that—an imposter.'** [Quran 68:11–13] If you want, we will pardon you this time, but do not return." The man said, "Pardon me, and I will not return again, O Commander of the Believers." A believer who takes Allah's Law ﷻ as the authority and acts according to His revelation responds in this way. This closes the door for people who wish to disparage and slander others.

On the other hand, when the ears are attentive to useless speech and slander, this increases the likelihood of sin. These words become ravenous predators and devastating weapons that wreak havoc on society. Such statements disrupt the cohesion between people's hearts and weaken their faith (*īmān*). This threat spreads when receptive ears listen to such evil.

The great Companion, 'Abd-Allah ibn 'Umar ﵄ was once walking with his freed slave, Nāfi'. He heard a forbidden instrument, the flute, being played, so Ibn 'Umar ﵄ plugged his ears with his fingers and began walking in a different direction. He asked his freed slave, "Do you still hear it?" He said, "Yes." He kept his fingers in his ears until Nāfi' said that he could no longer hear it, after which he unplugged his ears and returned to the path. He said, "This is what I saw the Messenger of Allah ﷺ do."[23] He chose this dignified response hoping that Allah ﷻ would address him honorably and he would enjoy the melodies of Paradise that He grants those who avoid listening to forbidden things in this fleeting life.

This example illustrates the risk associated with what we listen to. By listening to things that are forbidden in the Sharia, a person exposes himself to having molten lead poured into his ears. This is a type of punishment that the Messenger of Allah ﷺ informed us of, reserved for certain crimes related to hearing, such as eavesdropping.[24]

REFINING HEARING

The exalted Sharia has organized, systematized, and stabilized the foundations of our actions so that people preserve their honor and avoid ruin. One such forbidden action is eavesdropping, which consists of

---

23 Narrated by Ibn Ḥibbān in his *Ṣaḥīḥ*, and by Ibn Abī al-Dunyā in his chapter On Scrupulousness.

24 Narrated by al-Bukhārī in *Kitāb al-Ta'bīr* (Hadith 6635) and the Hadith is as follows, *"Whoever narrates a dream that he did not actually see, he will be forced ⸢on the Day of Resurrection⸣ to join two grains of barley—and he will not be able to. Whoever listens to a group's conversation without their consent* (or *"after they distanced themselves from him"*)*, molten lead is poured into his ears on the Day of Resurrection. Whoever makes an image is punished and forced to blow ⸢a soul⸣ into it, and he cannot do so."*

overhearing a group's conversation without their consent. What do you expect from such a conversation? What do you expect to get from prying into people's secrets? Or from inquiring about things that they do not want you to know about? The Sharia honors the right to privacy so much so that if someone talks to you about something, then turns around out of fear that someone might overhear, everything you heard must be treated as completely confidential.[25]

People's mindfulness of Allah ﷻ has diminished in this regard, so it is necessary to cultivate our awareness of Allah in relation to the things we hear, such as news, stories, or conversations about both people living and deceased. We are prohibited from listening to someone insulting a Muslim, whether they are alive or dead. The one insulting another Muslim is committing a crime and the person listening is his accomplice. The Prophet ﷺ told us to do the opposite, *"Recall the good qualities of your dead, and refrain from ⸢mentioning⸣ their shortcomings."*[26] This specifically applies to the dead, but also applies in a general sense to the living as well. One of the Companions asked, "O Messenger of Allah, what if what I say about my brother is true?" He said, *"If what you say is true, then it is backbiting; and if it what you say is not true, then you have slandered him."* Slander, defamation, and fabricating lies are even worse than backbiting.

It is necessary for every person to be selective of what he listens to because hearing is a door to his heart. We previously mentioned a noble verse of the Quran that connects the faculties of hearing and sight to the heart, **"Indeed, hearing, sight, and the heart—you will be questioned about all of these."** [Quran 17:36] In the following verse, Allah ﷻ mentions the distinction of the hearing of those who recognized and believed in the truth, **"When they listen to what has been revealed**

25 This refers to the Hadith narrated by Aḥmad, that Jābir ibn ʿAbd-Allāh ﷺ heard the Prophet ﷺ say: *"If a person speaks and looks around, then it is a trust."*

26 Narrated by Abū Dawūd, al-Tirmidhī, al-Ḥākim in *al-Mustadrak*, and al-Bayhaqī in his *Sunan* on the authority of Ibn ʿUmar.

to the Messenger, you see their eyes flowing with tears because they recognize the truth." [Quran 5:83]

He also said ﷻ, **"And when they hear frivolous talk, they turn away from it, saying, 'Peace be with you! We want nothing to do with the ignorant.'"** [Quran 28:55]

He ﷻ also said, **"And when the foolish address them, they reply with, 'Peace!'"** [Quran 25:63]

On the other hand, Allah ﷻ tells us how the people of evil and falsehood distance themselves from listening to the people of virtue, preferring evil speech instead: **"The disbelievers said ⌜to one another⌝, 'Do not listen to this Quran, but drown it out."** [Quran 41:26] The degree of a person's receptivity to Quranic counsel is in accordance with the degree of faith in his heart.

O Allah, fill our hearts with the lights of being in awe of You, of turning to You, of anticipating the meeting with You, and of having proper manners with You. Fill our hearts with that which guarantees us felicity in both worlds—by Your mercy, O Most Merciful! May Allah send peace and blessings upon the Chosen One, Muhammad, and his Family and Companions. All praise belongs to Allah, Lord of the Worlds.

CHAPTER 6

Listening to Advice

All praise belongs to Allah, the All-Hearing, All-Knowing, All-Powerful. There is no god other than Him. The beginning is from Him, and the ultimate end is to Him. He sent His chosen servant Muhammad to us—the deliverer of good news, the warner, and the luminous lamp. May Allah send His peace, blessings, and mercy upon him, his Family, Companions, and all those who follow his path until the Day of Judgment.

To proceed: The One who gave us our hearing, sight, and hearts encourages us to feel the onus to be grateful to Him by admonishing those who lack gratitude when He سبحانه وتعالى said, **"And He gave you hearing, sight, and hearts. ⌜Yet⌝ you hardly give any thanks."** [Quran 32:9] This verse indicates that most people do not use these great gifts and blessings for the purpose for which they were created, nor do they use them in ways that benefit them inwardly and outwardly in this life and the next. It also shows us that most people use these blessings to disobey Allah سبحانه وتعالى, the One who granted them these gifts and gave them control over these faculties.

THE OBLIGATION OF GRATITUDE TO ALLAH ﷻ

As the possessor of this vast Kingdom, you should be aware that all the technological devices that people are impressed by are only the products of the original divine gifts given to humanity, **"Though most people do not know."** [Quran 7:187] **"But most people are ungrateful."** [Quran 2:243] It is incumbent upon everyone who believes in the Giver of these gifts to be completely grateful to Him ﷻ. We must use these capacities to attain our Creator's good pleasure. In doing so, one finds glory, honor, and nobility. This gives people steadfastness in this world and prepares them for everlasting blessings and an endless Kingdom. **"This is Allah's favor, which He bestows on whomever He pleases."** [Quran 57:21]

Using hearing and sight properly leads to the extremely significant matter of having uprightness in contemplation and reflection, in taking and giving, in turning to Allah ﷻ, and in meeting the standard set by the Messenger of Allah ﷺ in dealing with all types of people.

An example of someone properly using the faculty of hearing is that when he receives advice or an error of his is brought to his attention, he happily acknowledges it. Welcoming advice reflects a person's awareness of the right Allah has over him and of the greatness of the return to Him ﷻ. It is along these lines that ʿUmar ibn al-Khaṭṭāb ؓ, a person who was taught directly by the Prophet ﷺ, said, "May Allah have mercy on whoever gifts me my flaws."[27]

The Companions loved to lend their ears to counsel (*naṣīḥa*), and they would seek counsel from their brothers and those lesser than them by requesting that they observe their behavior. They were able to do this because their intentions were pure, their inner state was unblemished, and they understood their purpose in life. They anticipated standing before Allah Most High ﷻ for His judgment. If Allah grants someone felicity, they will have enduring bliss; but if He decrees wretchedness

27 Narrated by al-Daylamī in his *Sunan*.

for someone, their misery will be never-ending—and we seek refuge in Allah ﷻ from that.

BENEFITTING FROM COUNSEL

ʿUmar ibn al-Khaṭṭāb's statement, "May Allah have mercy on whoever gifts me my flaws," is an example of someone using their hearing properly and genuinely welcoming counsel, because it is a gift from the one giving counsel. Regardless of what the person giving counsel might have intended, you can benefit from him. Intelligent people use their hearing to benefit even from the words of those who oppose and envy them, taking whatever might give them insight into rectifying a flaw or shortcoming within themselves. They are not concerned with the envy, loathing, or arrogance that the other person might be harboring in his heart. The intelligent person is self-critical. Allah ﷻ said, **"Truly, a person is a clear witness against himself, despite the excuses he may come up with."** [Quran 75:14–15] He benefits from the situation and employs his hearing in a way that benefits him in this life and the next.

One of the most significant manifestations of using one's hearing properly relates to sincere counsel (*naṣīḥa*), which encompasses the entire religion, as mentioned in the statement of the Prophet Muhammad ﷺ, *"The essence of the religion is in being sincere."* The Companions asked, "With whom?" He said, *"With Allah, His Book, His Messenger, and the leaders and generality of the Muslims."*[28]

The meaning of *naṣīḥa* in the Hadith has many meanings. When we apply it to hearing specifically, it encompasses all that relates to hearing about Allah's attributes and exaltedness ﷻ; the attributes of His Messenger ﷺ, his life, character, traits, and noble guidance; and the Quran, its recitation, rulings, and virtues as a whole and of specific

28 Muslim in *Kitāb al-Īmān* (Hadith 55).

Sūras or verses. It also relates to hearing about Muslim leaders, which could apply to scholars or governing authorities.

Regarding scholars, we should listen to words that increase our reverence for people of virtue, knowledge, and piety. With regard to governing authorities, we listen to words that teach us how to treat our leaders well in order to be protected from chaos, to avoid approving what Allah ﷻ has made forbidden, and to be safe from withholding anyone's rights (which must be achieved in ways that are sound and upright). We also listen to what relates to the state of society regarding what benefits the individual, the family, and the community. Heeding reminders in all these areas is considered part of listening to *naṣīḥa.*

We began by specifically mentioning *listening to counsel* as part of *naṣīḥa*. This relates to each of us individually when someone notices something about us, brings it to our attention, or advises us with regard to our actions or speech.

Although people's intentions may vary when giving counsel, the one receiving counsel should nevertheless accept it with excellence, regardless of who is giving it. He does so by reflecting on what was said about him, reminding himself to establish Allah's command, and using the counsel to improve his own state. A person is often unaware of certain things within himself that others may see. This is further demonstrated in the Hadith, *"The believer is another believer's mirror."*[29] Using our hearing in the ways mentioned above then serves a beautiful purpose.

THE EFFECT OF GOOD COUNSEL ON THE UMMAH

The righteous Companions, Followers (*Tabiʿīn*), and those after them would seek out counsel and direction from others in hopes of correcting any deficiencies they may have had. They did this because they knew

29 Narrated by Abū Dawūd on the authority of Abū Hurayra with a sound (*ḥasan*) chain.

that by doing so, they were fulfilling one of the duties of servitude (*ʿubūdīyyah*), which leads to distinction, bliss, and Allah's good pleasure. This is why they actively sought advice from others.

Allah ﷻ made mutual counsel one of the foundations for being saved from loss. He ﷻ said, **"By the ⌜passage of⌝ time! Surely, man is in ⌜grave⌝ loss! Except for those who believe, do good deeds, urge one another to the truth, and urge one another to steadfastness."** [Quran 103:1–3] Urging one another in this way, which requires attentive ears and receptive hearts, remedies people's deficiencies and corrects their alignment. When each of the actions within this Kingdom are properly utilized, people increase in beauty, excellence, and splendor. Therefore, one of the functions of your hearing is to listen to other people's critique of you in hopes of being granted the lofty station of the All-Merciful's good pleasure ﷻ.

The great Companions ʿUmar ibn al-Khaṭṭāb and Salmān al-Fārisī ؓ met after they had been apart for a long time. ʿUmar asked, "What have you heard about me that you dislike?" Salmān said, "I ask to be excused from answering this question, O Commander of the Believers." When ʿUmar insisted, Salmān said, "I have heard that you wear two outfits on the same day and that you have two types of sauce at the same meal." ʿUmar then asked, "Is there anything else besides these two things?" to which Salmān said, "No." ʿUmar then said, "As for these two things, I hereby refrain from them." In other words, I hear your advice and will heed what you say, so after today I will not have two types of sauce at one meal nor wear two outfits on the same day. ʿUmar's insistence in seeking advice from Salmān al-Fārisī ؓ shows the lessons that Messenger of Allah ﷺ embedded within them. What was ʿUmar's nature before becoming Muslim and following the Chosen One ﷺ? Before the Prophet ﷺ, would he have even accepted criticism, much less *seek out* counsel? Yet, these are the sublime stations attained by those who succeed in purifying their souls.

If there was true *naṣīḥa* among Muslims, this would bring about great good and ward off various afflictions, calamities, disputes, and other forms of evils that affect societies.

We also need to extensively listen to the Book of Allah سبحانه وتعالى. We should never deprive our ears from listening to our Lord's speech each day and night. We should have a daily portion that we recite with reflection and contemplation. Allah سبحانه وتعالى said, **"When the Quran is recited, listen to it attentively and be silent, so that you may be shown mercy."** [Quran 7:204] Every believer should use each of their limbs for the purpose for which they were created, directing their actions in obedience to Allah سبحانه وتعالى, thereby attaining felicity in both abodes.

We ask Allah to guide us to what pleases Him, and we ask Him to make us steadfast upon what He loves in what we say, listen to, and convey—He is the Most Generous of all. May Allah send peace and blessings upon the Chosen One, Muhammad, and upon his Family and Companions. All praise belongs to Allah, Lord of the Worlds.

CHAPTER 7

Sight & Inner Sight

All praise belongs to Allah, vast in Gentleness, Knower of the apparent and hidden. There is no god but Him, the One, the Singular. He sent His Beloved to us, the Chosen One, Muhammad, with the way of right guidance. O Allah, send peace and blessings upon Your Servant, the Elected One who guides people to You, our master Muhammad, and upon his pure Family, his most excellent Companions, and all those who follow their way.

To proceed: Allah ﷻ created our eyesight, so we need to use this faculty properly to observe the vast meanings that Allah ﷻ has unfolded in His creation. We must guard it and the Kingdom of the Heart against anything that will cause us regret in the Hereafter. When our vision is used properly it connects to our inner sight (*baṣīra*)[30] and we then comprehend realities and ultimate ends, as well as the consequences of words and actions. These things show us the significance of eyesight.

30 Translator's note: The Arabic word for eyesight is *baṣar* and for inner sight is *baṣīra*, and there is a linguistic relation between the two.

THE EFFECT OF EYESIGHT ON THE INNER SIGHT

We hear in many verses of the Quran the command 'to look' and 'to see' coupled with reflection, consideration, and contemplation. This shows us that when we use our eyesight properly, it connects to our inner sight. This inner sight is so valuable that if a person loses it, he loses his divinely given distinction, becoming truly 'blind.' The following verses give us insights into the meaning of inner sight, **"But whoever turns away from My Reminder will certainly have a miserable life, then We will raise him up blind on the Day of Resurrection. He will say, 'My Lord! Why have you raised me up blind, although I used to see?' Allah will say, 'Just as Our revelations came to you and you neglected them, so today you are neglected.'"** [Quran 20:124–126]

Allah ﷻ also said, **"But whoever is blind ⌜to the truth⌝ in this life will be blind in the Hereafter, and even more astray from the path."** [Quran 17:72]

"Can you make the deaf hear, or guide the blind or those who are clearly astray?" [Quran 43:40]

"Indeed, it is not the eyes that are blind, but it is the hearts within the chests." [Quran 22:46] In other words, a person who has lost his eyesight is not impaired so long as his heart is illuminated.

This teaches us the reality of 'blindness' and 'vision.' The purpose of our eyesight is for it to connect to inner sight, and that the former is of secondary importance to the latter. Allah ﷻ said, **"Can the one who knows that your Lord's revelation to you ⌜O Prophet⌝ is the truth be like the one who is blind? Only those with understanding will take heed."** [Quran 13:19]

Whoever lacks conviction in his heart that what was revealed to Muhammad ﷺ from Allah ﷻ is the truth is blind. By this measure, you see how widespread this dangerous form of blindness is within the Ummah—that most people are blind to the path of guidance and have not benefitted from their eyesight. Had they used their sight properly, it would have led to the illumination of their inner sight. They would have come to know the reality of this existence: that it has an Exalted and Unique Creator ﷾, that the end is to Him, and what He has revealed is the truth. He sent His Messengers to save people, take them out of depths of darkness into the light, and show them Allah's guidance and path ﷾.

THE IMPACT OF LOOKING AT FORBIDDEN THINGS

You have been blessed with eyesight, so are you aware that every gaze that transgresses your Lord's commands scars your heart? This includes every evil, scornful, or harmful look directed at another Muslim. Every time you look to find the flaws of another Muslim or peer inside a person's house without permission scars your heart. Do you not know that this evil veils you from the realities of felicity, whether you perceive this or not? *"Whoever seeks out the flaws of his Muslim brother, Allah seeks out his flaws and exposes him, even if he is in the privacy of his own home."*[31]

Likewise, when you look with desire at someone who is impermissible for you to look at, this darkens the heart and blinds the inner sight, detracts from one's honor, and becomes a source of regret on the Day of Resurrection. The Quran commands us, **"⸢O Prophet⸣, tell the believing men to lower their gaze and guard their chastity—that is purer for them. Allah is well aware of what they do. And tell the believing women to lower their gaze and guard their chastity, and not to reveal their adornments beyond what normally appears and let them draw their veils over their chests."** [Quran 24:30–31] Allah ﷾ told His Prophet to speak to the *believers* because only a believer would understand why he must lower his gaze. A non-believer would ask why he must refrain from looking at something his lower self (*nafs*) enjoys.

31 A noble Hadith narrated by al-Bayhaqī in *Shuʿab al-Īmān*.

The believer, on the other hand, understands. Allah concludes the verse with a perspective of faith that allows the believer to understand *why* he must lower his gaze, "**˹O Prophet˺, tell the believing men to lower their gaze and guard their chastity—that is purer for them. *Allah is all aware of what they do.***" [Quran 24:30] The believer is accountable to the One who is All-Aware of His creation, which is why he must avert his gaze from everything Allah ﷻ has forbidden him to look at.

The Prophet ﷺ said, *"It is enough evil for a person to look down on his Muslim brother."*[32] He taught us to recognize the wisdom in the creation of all things, whether they be plants, animals, or inanimate objects. The Prophet ﷺ commanded us to witness the wisdom in its creation, and that by doing so, we no longer look at others with disdain. To look down on others is an internal flaw that scars our inner sight and harms us.

RECTIFYING ONE'S EYESIGHT

A believer must use his vision to ponder and reflect on the cosmos and fulfill his religious and worldly needs both inwardly and outwardly. He should prevent himself from looking at people's deficiencies or from gazing desirously at someone he is not permitted to look at. This cultivates his inner sight and brings peace to his heart.

A poet once said,

Every calamity begins with a gaze
Just as a small spark starts the fire's blaze
So long as a man looks about haphazardly
At fair maidens—then he is in jeopardy

The more you look at things with desire, the more difficulties you face and the more the fire rages in your heart. Looking at these things means

32 Narrated by Muslim in *Kitāb al-Birr* (Hadith 2546).

disobeying the Overpowering One, which exposes us to punishment in the life to come. So it is crucial for you to control your gaze.

Allah gave us our vision to allow our inner sight to witness His Magnificence ﷻ. He says, **"Say, 'Look at what is in the heavens and on the earth.' But what use are signs and warnings to people who will not believe?"** [Quran 10:101] And, **"Have they not travelled throughout the land to see how those before them met their end? Allah annihilated them, and a similar fate awaits the disbelievers."** [Quran 47:10]

It is extremely dangerous for us to look at things that arouse our desire. Doing so immediately brings trouble and exposes us to punishment in the life to come. It is in our best interests to prevent ourselves from looking at what Allah ﷻ has made forbidden. Amazingly, when a person averts his gaze from what is forbidden, he receives an immediate reward that he experiences in this world before the next. The Prophet ﷺ said in a Hadith, *"The lustful gaze is a poisonous arrow from the quiver of Iblīs. Allah says, '**When someone resists it out of fear of Me, I replace it with faith, the sweetness of which he finds in his heart.**'"*[33] This means that Allah ﷻ immediately allows him to taste the sweetness of faith to the degree to which he averts his gaze from what He has made forbidden.

You possess the Kingdom of sight. If you truly were vigilant of Allah ﷻ, the All-Hearing and All-Seeing, in how you use your eyes, you will look upon the faces of the Prophets, the Entirely True (*Ṣiddiqūn*), the martyrs, and the righteous on the Day of Resurrection and in the Abode of Honor. But if you tainted your sight by looking at other's deficiencies and forbidden things, then you are at risk of losing out on seeing these people in the Hereafter. In that case, you will only see the dust-covered faces of the disbelievers and the wicked, and you will gaze at the punishment of the Fire—and we seek refuge in Allah from that.

Instead, prepare your eyes to look at the face of the Prophet

33 Narrated by al-Ḥākim who classified it as authentic on the authority of Ḥudhayfa, and by al-Ṭabarānī on the authority of Ibn Masʿūd.

Muhammad ﷺ as he carries the Banner of Praise on the Day of Resurrection. You can only see this by averting your gaze from forbidden things and by being selective of what you look at. Someone who is selective knows how to control what he looks at, whether in a newspaper or magazine, on a screen, or otherwise. A person who makes good decisions about what he looks at sets himself up for everlasting bliss and a great portion of Allah's favors in this life and the next.

O Allah, employ our eyesight and hearing in that which guarantees us honor and dignity in this life and the next. Prevent these faculties from causing us remorse and painful punishment. O Living and Self-Subsistent, make us people who are selective of what we listen to and look at, so that we may be rewarded in this life and in the Everlasting Abode—by Your mercy, O Most Merciful! May Allah's peace and blessings be upon our master Muhammad, his Family, and his Companions. All praise belongs to Allah, Lord of the Worlds.

CHAPTER 8

Looking at Creation with Love & Mercy

All praise belongs to Allah, the All-Hearing, All-Seeing, Most Subtle, All-Aware, All-Knowing, and All-Powerful. There is no god but Him, One without partner. The Kingdom is His and all praise belongs to Him. He causes life and death, and He has power over all things. He sent us His servant Muhammad ﷺ as a bearer of good news, a warner, a caller to Him, a guide, and a luminous lamp. O Allah, send Your endless blessings upon Your Chosen Servant, our master Muhammad, and upon his Family, Companions, and all those who follow his path.

To proceed: By using the blessing of eyesight in a way that is pleasing to Allah ﷻ, you attain high degrees and great rewards.

You have been blessed with eyesight and your thousands and millions of receptor cells convey images to your consciousness, which allows you to comprehend many things. So be mindful of the One who created your eyesight and gave it to you. Be vigilant of the way that you manage and direct your sight. Are you using it according to what He has ordained for you in the Sacred Law? Or are you defying the One who gave you this blessing by using it in ways that He has forbidden and warned you against?

EYESIGHT AND WORSHIP

Our eyesight greatly influences our worship. For example, when a person is praying, he must avoid looking around because focusing his gaze is more conducive to having presence of heart and attaining the reality of the Prayer. This is what is indicated in His Words ﷻ, **"Successful indeed are the believers! Those who humble themselves in their Prayer."** [Quran 23:1–2] We are encouraged to look at the place of prostration (*sujūd*) and avoid looking at anything to the right or left. Some scholars even say that if you can identify the person praying to the right or left of you, you have not humbled yourself in prayer. The Prophet ﷺ said, *"People must stop looking up in Prayer or else their eyesight will be taken from them."*[34] He ﷺ also said about those who look to the left and right during the Prayer, *"It is a glance by which Satan steals from the servant's Prayer"*[35]—meaning the servant's reward from the Prayer is diminished.

Similarly, with fasting we find that if a fasting person looks at something that Allah ﷻ has forbidden, he misses out on the reality, spirit, and purpose of the fast. It is narrated that, *"Five things break a person's fast: lying, backbiting, talebearing, false testimony, and a lustful gaze."*[36] His reward for fasting, which is distinct from the reward for any other act of worship, is lost and the fast has no impact on him. The Prophet ﷺ said, *"Every good deed is multiplied by ten to seven-hundred times, and even more. Allah the Exalted has said, '**Except for fasting—it is Mine and I give its due. A person leaves his food, drink, and desire for My sake.**'"*[37]

We mentioned previously that Allah ﷻ gives the person who averts his gaze from looking at something forbidden an immediate reward,

---

34 Narrated by Muslim in *Kitāb al-Ṣalāh* (Hadith 428, 429).

35 Narrated by al-Bukhārī in *Kitāb Ṣifa al-Ṣalāh* (Hadith 718).

36 Narrated by al-Daylamī on the authority of Anas. Al-Azdī categorized it as weak (*daʿīf*).

37 Narrated by Aḥmad on the authority of Abū Hurayra, and by al-Bayhaqī in *Shuʿab al-Imān.*

allowing him to experience the sweetness of faith. As mentioned in the Hadith, ***"I replace it with faith, the sweetness of which he finds in his heart."***[38] This 'sweetness' is more desirable to people of knowledge and insight than every forbidden gaze and desire. It is more pleasurable than those things that appear to be desirable but actually have terrible effects.

We must regulate our eyesight so that it conforms to Allah's command, the Truly Great ﷻ. If we do so, our state when praying or fasting improves and we truly perform that act of worship as Allah ﷻ intended. This makes it possible for a person to attain great rewards when fasting, performing the Hajj, or other acts of worship.

Allah ﷻ has made it easy for us to avoid looking at something impermissible by simply closing our eyes. Since Allah has blessed you with eyesight, it is only fitting that you do this simple thing to avoid what He has forbidden. This is a necessary part of your duty as a human being and servant of the All-Merciful ﷻ.

We must take the proper approach when using our eyesight so that we use it in a way that benefits us in this life and the next. Whoever yearns to see the blessings, gifts, and maidens of Paradise, then it is only right that he refrains from looking at what his Lord ﷻ has made forbidden and uses his sight in a way that is beneficial.

LOOKING WITH MERCY AND RESPECT

Let us now address another of the aspect of sight, which is to look at all Muslims with mercy, respect, and reverence. This kind of gaze has a great impact on people's hearts and relationships. Smiling at another believer is a charity because it engenders love and fills the heart with positive emotions. By extension, looking at a believer with mercy, respect, and reverence is a means for attaining great rewards. It immediately impacts

38 Narrated by al-Ḥākim which he classified as authentic on the authority of Ḥudhayfa, and by al-Ṭabarānī on the authority of Ibn Masʿūd.

people's relationships, produces love within families, and spreads positivity and goodness within societies. Since it is considered sufficient evil to look at a fellow Muslim with scorn, then it is sufficient good to revere another Muslim and to look at him with mercy, compassion, and affection.

Few people are aware of this, and this has caused them to miss out on a lot of good related to brotherhood, marriage, and with their children and parents. If looking with gentleness and compassion is lost in these relationships, it upsets the family's balance, stability, and cohesion. We must therefore make it a habit to look with mercy and love at all Muslims generally, and especially our relatives, neighbors, friends, and community members. Doing so benefits the family and society and even impacts the way people interact with one another in worldly dealings.

ITS IMPACT ON SOCIETY

When looking this way at people becomes widespread, it has a significant impact on people's hearts and produces a spirit of giving sincere counsel to, wanting benefit for, and bringing happiness to others. We should therefore not neglect this type of gaze. We should be aware that part of our servitude to Allah ﷻ is to look at Muslims with mercy—those around us, those whose company we keep, and those whom we speak to.

The impact of this gaze can be felt as soon as someone looks at you. Those who exude mercy sometimes captivate you with their first glance and you become intensely drawn to them as soon as you look at each other. Looking at people with mercy and compassion provides them with much needed healing. However, it requires continuous consolidation and reinforcement. You might not see an effect the first time you look at someone in this way, but consistently doing this has an impact that will become apparent over time.

We cannot neglect looking at someone with gentleness, mercy, and compassion, even when that person falls into wrongdoing. Looking at him with mercy is part of the solution and becomes a way to set him back on the right path. Even when an individual is deserving of censure or punishment, do not stop looking at him with mercy so as not to assist the devil against him. When someone insulted a man who was being punished for drinking alcohol, the Prophet ﷺ rebuked him, saying, *"Do not be an ally to the Devil against your brother."*[39] In other words, we establish the punishments as a means of salvation, felicity, and raising of rank—not to humiliate people, run them into the ground, or take vengeance against them. We need to establish the punishment (*ḥadd*) to raise their rank, restore them to goodness, and create a barrier between them and that which harms them. This is all intended to help make them upright. Likewise, looking at others with mercy serves the same purpose.

When we look at others in this way while we are fasting, we enhance our fast, and the same applies to other righteous actions. Although these acts of worship are enriched by properly using our eyesight, they originate from the heart, and acts of worship from the heart have an immense reward with Allah ﷻ. Many are unaware that these actions are even rewarded by Allah, but they are in fact exalted acts of devotion: looking with compassion at all Muslims, looking at one's parents and grandparents with respect and reverence specifically, and looking with mercy at one's children, siblings, and others. This is one of the ways to mend relationships between Muslims and is a way to heal and guide many people.

May Allah ﷻ make us of those who look with excellence so that those we look at become well-pleased with Him inwardly and outwardly. May He instill compassion, mercy, and respect for Muslims within our hearts, which then rectifies our gaze so that we constantly look at others with gentleness, mercy, and compassion. May we attain the fruits of this

39 Narrated by Ibn 'Abd al-Barr in *al-Istī'āb*.

noble action in this life and in the next—O Most Merciful! May Allah's peace and blessings be upon our master Muhammad, his Family, and his Companions. All praise belongs to Allah, Lord of the Worlds.

CHAPTER 9

Reflecting on Creation & Understanding our Responsibility

All praise belongs to Allah, the Supreme Patron, the Creator of all things, the One to whom all will return—**"Your Lord will certainly judge between them on the Day of Resurrection regarding their differences."** [Quran 10:93] O Allah, send your peace and blessings upon our master Muhammad, our Guide to the right way, and upon his Family, Companions, and those who follow his path and embody his noble character and etiquettes. May we be counted with them and among them by Your mercy, O Most Generous Bestower.

To proceed: The uses, impact, and outcomes of how we use our eyesight are vast. An important aspect of our vision is how it should be used to observe and comprehend all that we see. When someone has a deep understanding, he is able to benefit from everything he sees. He knows when to lower his gaze and when to look around, thus benefitting in each and every situation. Whenever he looks at something, he perceives the wisdom of its creation and the fact that it points to something greater.

Allah ﷻ commands us, **"Contemplate on what is in the heavens and on the earth."** [Quran 10:101]

And, **"Have they not contemplated the realm of the heavens and**

earth and all that Allah created, and that perhaps the end of their time might be near?" [Quran 7:185]

Each thing created by Allah contains proofs, meanings, and signs for the people of discernment. But when a person is engulfed in heedlessness, he apathetically turns away from the signs. Allah ﷾ said, **"There are many signs in the heavens and the earth that they pass by with indifference!"** [Quran 12:105]

As Muslims, we must remember to use our eyesight to contemplate the cosmos and ponder its signs, which point to the Exaltedness of the Creator ﷾. This can be accomplished by looking at the wonders of plants or the amazing diversity of land and sea creatures. There are many nature programs that document these signs, yet some people watch them only to be entertained, remaining oblivious of their connection to the Creator who created all these things from water through His expansive power ﷾.

CONTEMPLATING THE CREATOR'S EXALTEDNESS ﷾

Contemplating the marvels in creation should deepen our connection to the Creator's exaltedness, power, and will. Allah's signs in creation are reminders of our return to Him ﷾. Let us reflect on the wonders on land and sea, in the heavens, and within our own selves. Allah ﷾ said, **"There are signs on the earth for those with certitude, as there are within your own selves. Can you not see? In heaven is your sustenance and whatever you are promised. Then, by the Lord of the heaven and earth! This is certainly as true as the ˹fact that˺ you can speak!"** [Quran 51:20–23] Using our vision in this way increases our faith and certitude in the One, the Real, the Originator ﷾.

We should reflect on the splendid and flawless order of the cosmos. **"You will not see any imperfection in the All-Merciful's creation. Look again! Can you see any flaw? Then look again and again—your sight will return weak and weary."** [Quran 67:3–4] You will find signs and wisdoms in all His creation, and you will see the marvels of His excellent arranging and planning ﷻ.

Think of how many marvels are present within the bee and its hive! Similarly, you see such wonders in the ant and the arrangement of its colony. When we look at these things to see Allah's signs, this benefits us immensely and strengthens our belief in Allah ﷻ. We must accustom ourselves, in our day-to-day lives, to look with contemplation at the things that surround us. This form of contemplation should take precedence whenever we watch a film that shows us something of the wonders of the constellations, creatures on land or in the sea, or anything else that serves as evidence of Allah's power ﷻ.

A Muslim teacher who teaches geology or astronomy is duty-bound to connect the subject matter to Allah's exaltedness, power, and our ultimate return to Him. The teacher should instill hope in and fear of Allah within students and the aspiration to seek His good pleasure ﷻ. These are some of the duties of teachers specifically, and more broadly, of people who are fascinated by the wonders of the heavens and earth. When teaching others, they should use the Prophet's didactic method ﷺ. His way of speaking about the cosmos instilled within people's hearts a veneration for the One Who created and perfectly fashioned them ﷻ. This area contains great potential for those who seek to truly see. This aspect of eyesight helps us acquire greater degrees and lofty ranks. We achieve this by looking at and pondering what the Creator of our sight ﷻ has called us to contemplate.

When someone mentioned the proof of Allah's existence to a Bedouin man, he responded saying, "Footprints are an indication that a traveler has passed, and droppings are an indication that a camel has passed. So do not heavens filled with constellations, an earth filled with valleys, and seas with crashing waves point to the existence of the All-Knowing Creator?"

This type of contemplation yields many benefits. Allah ﷻ addresses the disbelievers regarding some of the marvels in creation, saying, **"Do the disbelievers not realize that the heavens and earth were once one mass, then We split them apart?"** [Quran 21:30] In some cases, disbelievers are the ones to make these discoveries because Muslims have neglected their duty and only care about their individual interests. This has become so dominant that many people do not even think about what benefits society or what benefits the Ummah, with rare exception. We *must* rise above this level.

CONTEMPLATING THE STATE OF THE UMMAH

We must raise the awareness of our individual, and especially communal, duty to contemplate the current state of the Ummah, its future, and what benefits it the most. Every believer must know that he has a part to play in benefitting the Ummah. Being confined by greed, seeking only personal gains, and chasing worldly ambitions has caused us to fall behind in discovering the marvels of creation and uncovering the realities of existence. Allah ﷻ said, **"We will show them Our signs in the universe and within themselves until it becomes clear that this is the Truth. Is it not enough that your Lord is a Witness over all things?"** [Quran 41:53]

Regrettably, we raise children to be concerned only with personal gains and fleeting pleasures. The child learns this from his family members who live this way. No one motivates him to benefit the Ummah, spread goodness, or help rectify people's character. This only holds a child back and limits him, whereas the child might consider this flawed approach to be the peak of intelligence. The child focuses only on acquiring material wealth because that is what he sees so-called cultured, ambitious, and sophisticated people do. The inversion of values and the misuse of the blessing of vision are what have brought this about. This has had an adverse effect on people's inner sight, causing realities to become inverted and falsehood to surface. This has affected our lives, our capability to realize our goals, and our relationship with the societies and time in which we live.

There are many people who do not live long, but they were concerned for the Ummah and recognized their responsibility towards it. As a result, Allah ﷻ made them sources of great good, not just during their lifetimes but long after they died. They were not deceived by the world's adornments. Instead, they perceived the true meaning of this world and learned from the different states of people. They understood their immense responsibility in life.

On the other hand, there are many people who accumulated wealth and sought worldly titles but have now vanished. Their names have been forgotten and their lives have passed, but they never accomplished a meaningful goal nor attained any rank with Allah. They are gone, and all that they had is gone with them. A person's destiny is based on what he did and how he used his life, which might appear to have been long, but was of little value.

O Allah, grant us true understanding of what is pleasing to You. Rectify our eyesight and inner sight in a way that raises us in rank and allows us to recognize the obligation to serve the Ummah and benefit creation—O Beneficent, Most-Generous, and Benevolent! May Allah's peace and blessings be upon our master Muhammad, and upon his Family and Companions. All praise belongs to Allah, Lord of the Worlds.

CHAPTER 10

The Impact of Shaking Hands on the Heart & Society

All praise belongs to Allah, the All-Powerful Sovereign, the Gatherer of creation on the Last Day. There is no god but Him, One without partner. He sent His Servant Muhammad, the Chosen One, with guidance and the religion of truth to make it prevail over all others, even though the polytheists may hate it. May Allah's peace and blessings be upon him, his Family and Companions, and upon whoever follows his guidance and path until the Day of Reckoning.

To proceed: When we look at the Quran, we find that the acquisition of deeds is attributed to the hands, as Allah سبحانه وتعالى says, **". . .it is because of what your hands have done,"** [Quran 42:30] and **"what their hands have done,"** [Quran 36:35] and **"this is on account of what your hands have done."** [Quran 3:182] This shows that our hands have an important role in bringing about actions and allowing us to achieve things. When we fulfill a need or achieve a goal, we use our hands. This is why the entirety of person's acquisition is attributed to their hands.

Given the importance of our hands, those who believe in Allah سبحانه وتعالى need to regulate their usage—whether in picking things up, touching and striking, weighing and measuring when buying and selling, raising and lowering, and grasping and letting go. The believer must ensure that he uses his inner sight when engaging in these things. He must be conscious that he is responsible for every movement that he makes, and that each action has consequences in this life and the next. These considerations make it necessary to focus on the hands.

THE IMPACT OF SHAKING HANDS ON THE HEART

The hands play a role in many spiritual and unseen matters that have wide-reaching ramifications on society. This is the reason why Islam teaches us to shake hands with other Muslims. Doing so benefits the heart by removing hatred from it. The Prophet ﷺ said, *"Shake hands with one another, for it removes hatred from your hearts."*[40] In reality, every outward action related to the body has a connection to the inward world of the heart. Shaking hands has an effect in unifying hearts and bringing them together, which is the wisdom in this Sunna. We were informed that it helps a believer maintain purity of heart towards others, which saves from disgrace on the Day of Resurrection. This is indicated in the Quran in the Intimate Friend Ibrāhīm's supplication, when he said to his Lord ﷻ, **"And do not disgrace me on the Day when people are resurrected—the Day when neither wealth nor children will be of any benefit. Except for those who come to Allah with a pure heart."** [Quran 26:87–89]

The loftiness and expansiveness of the Sharia regulates the way believers interact at gatherings, meetings, and when greeting one another. It is recommended to shake hands because it removes hatred, spreads harmony, and expresses the collective solidarity and cohesion between the ranks of Muslims. **"Allah truly loves those who fight in His cause in ranks, as if they were a tightly joined wall."** [Quran 61:4] It is also recommended to shake hands because it spreads true purity, love, and brotherhood. Shaking hands was given to us with these intended out-

40 Narrated by Ibn 'Adī from Ibn 'Umar, and by Mālik in the Muwaṭṭa'.

comes, and the Companions upheld this practice after being directed to do so by the Prophet ﷺ.

SHAKING HANDS WITH THE ANGELS

The Prophet ﷺ informed us that the Angels shake people's hands, which fosters great good within the hearts and purifies them. Angels shake hands with people, even if people do not see them, and they are in attendance when believers have gatherings of remembrance and Prayer.

It has even come in narration that the Angel Jibrīl ﷺ specifically shakes hands with some of those who pray and fast in Ramadan. The Prophet ﷺ said, *"Whoever feeds a fasting person in Ramadan, from a lawful income, the Angels pray for him throughout all the nights of Ramadan and Jibrīl shakes his hand on the Night of Great Worth* (Laylat al-Qadr). *And when Jibrīl ﷺ shakes a person's hand, that person's heart softens, and his tears increase."*[41] This results from shaking hands with Jibrīl ﷺ. The softening of one's heart is a reward for another action of the hands, which is feeding a fasting person.

This Hadith teaches us the virtue of feeding a fasting person. By way of your sacrifice and desire to perform this noble deed, you might be granted the honor of shaking hands with Jibrīl ﷺ. Though you do not see Jibrīl nor witness his form, it occurs as you are shaking hands with other people, Jibrīl's hand is coupled with their hands. The sign of this handshake becomes apparent as mentioned by the Prophet ﷺ when he said, *"When Jibrīl shakes a person's hand, that person's heart softens, and his tears increase."*

Look at what the hands acquire when we give of our wealth to feed fasting people sincerely for Allah's sake ﷻ (on the condition that we spend from purely acquired wealth as stated in the Hadith). The entire affair is connected to what the hands acquire. The hand that acquires

41 Narrated by Abū'l Shaykh on the authority of Salmān al-Fārisī.

permissible wealth and then spends it to feed a fasting person is preparing to shake hands with the one entrusted with revelation, the Angel Jibrīl ﷺ. This results in his heart softening and his tears increasing, which releases him from the shackles of hard-heartedness and heedlessness into the expansiveness of true faith. His heart then softens, and his eyes shed tears out of fear of the All-Merciful ﷻ. The Prophet ﷺ said, *"All eyes will be crying on the Day of Resurrection, except for eyes that looked away from what Allah the Glorious and Majestic forbade, eyes that stayed up at night in Allah's cause, and eyes that shed a tear even if it was as small as a fly's head out of fear of Allah the Glorious and Majestic."*[42]

Observe how things are interconnected and how that which is acquired by the hands impacts the heart and limbs. If a person's hands scrupulously acquire what is lawful and then spend that wealth in a way that Allah loves, the Angels will shake his hand, consequently affecting his heart and eyes. The eyes shed tears and the heart softens and is humbled. All this results from using the hands with excellence, thereby granting the hands an exalted status.

SHAKING HANDS WITH LOVE & ITS ETIQUETTES

Another aspect of shaking hands is that it expresses our love and respect for one another. The heart first experiences the meanings of love, brotherhood, and the bonds of faith. This is then expressed by shaking hands.

Some people may not experience these feelings, but it is hoped that shaking hands will have an effect on their hearts by removing any resentment they may have for others and by fostering fondness between them. We thus see that the dangerous diseases of greed, hatred, and resentment are treated by extending one's hand to a fellow Muslim.

For those whose hearts are not in need of treatment, shaking hands

42 Narrated by Abū Nu'aym in *al-Ḥilya* on the authority of Abū Hurayra with a sound (*ḥasan*) chain.

only affirms the praiseworthy attribute that has settled within their hearts and strengthens the connection that Allah ﷻ has placed between people of this great and magnanimous religion. We now see the great value of shaking hands. The Prophet ﷺ even said, *"Whenever two Muslims meet and shake hands, they are forgiven before they even go their separate ways."*[43]

When a person shakes hands with an elderly Muslim, their father or mother, or a person of knowledge, it is recommended that he kiss his or her hand. This was the state of the noble Companions ﷺ based on the teachings of the Prophet Muhammad ﷺ. When Thābit al-Bunānī would visit Anas ibn Mālik ﷺ, he would tell his maidservant, "Jamīla, pass me perfume to apply to my hands, because Thābit insists on kissing my hand." Thābit al-Bunānī would say, "This is a hand that touched the hand of the Messenger of Allah!"[44] He would shake his hand, then kiss it, envisioning how Anas's palm touched the palm of Allah's Beloved ﷺ. Look at how much the heart receives when experiencing these types of emotions and lofty meanings by way of righteous intentions.

On the contrary, the established ruling in the Sacred Law is that it is forbidden for a man to shake hands with a woman who is not a close relative, and vice versa. So this is something we must completely avoid. The Prophet ﷺ said in a narration, *"It is better for one of you to be poked in the head with a needle than for his hand to touch the hand of a woman who is forbidden to him."*[45] This is someone who is not one's spouse or non-marriageable relative.

This discussion shows how Islam in its vastness excellently directs each individual's actions. We all possess the vast Kingdom of the Heart, yet many people wrong themselves by being ignorant of the relationship between the heart and limbs. They lose out on the spiritual treasures of

---

43 Narrated by Abū Dawūd in *Kitab al-Adab* (Hadith 5212).

44 Narrated by Abū Yaʿlā, and mentioned by al-Dhahabī in *Siyar Aʿlām al-Nubalāʾ* in the fourth section.

45 Narrated by al-Ṭabarānī in *al-Kabīr*, and the narrators have the integrity of authentic (*Ṣaḥīḥ*) Hadith.

beauty, radiance, and dignity that adorn each of their limbs. Those who are heedless of Allah miss out on the special qualities of their actions. But when we follow the Prophet's Sunna ﷺ to bring us closer to Allah ﷻ and to benefit His creation and the Ummah, it has a great impact in adorning our deeds and giving them significance. Shaking hands is just one example of such an action. Through this one deed, brotherhood and love spread, and enmity and hatred dissipate.

O Allah, make our hands steadfastly upright upon that which pleases You, and make them engage in what will bring us happiness when we meet You in the Final Abode—O Lord of all creation, Most Generous, Bestower of Gifts! May peace and blessings be upon the Chosen One Muhammad, and his Family and Companions. All praise belongs to Allah, Lord of the Worlds.

CHAPTER 11

Scrupulously Avoiding Unlawful Things

All praise belongs to Allah, the most complete and perfect praise, in every state. May Allah's peace and blessings be upon the one sent with guidance, truth, light, and beauty: Muhammad ibn 'Abd-Allah, His choicest servant, and upon his Family and Companions, the best Companions and the best Family, and upon those who follow them with excellence until the Day when deeds are placed on the Scales.

To proceed: The realm of the hand's actions is vast and far-reaching. We previously mentioned some of the impact of shaking hands. Another important action of the hand that affects the faith and light within our hearts is refraining from taking what is unlawful. A person may have the opportunity to take something without its owner's knowledge and claim it as his own; but refraining from such an action leads to the attainment of the light of faith, which is of the loftiest and noblest types of light.

The light of faith continues to shine even when the light of the sun and moon are extinguished, **"When the sight is stunned, and the moon is dimmed, and the sun and moon are brought together."** [Quran 75:7–9] **"On that Day you will see the believing men and believing women with their light shining ahead of them and to their right."** [Quran 57:12]

A WARNING AGAINST BEING CARELESS OF OTHERS' RIGHTS

Taking that which is doubtful or forbidden without regard for the consequences may extinguish the light of faith and put someone at risk of dying outside the fold of Islam—and we seek refuge in Allah ﷻ from this.

A man was once in the throes of death, and as those around him were saying *"Lā ilāha illā Allāh"* to him, he was unable to say it. However, when they would speak about something else, he would converse with them. When this happened several times, someone present asked him, "Why do you become quiet when we say *'Lā ilāha illā Allāh'* but you speak when we talk about something else?!" He replied, "Whenever I want to say it, I feel my tongue being weighed down by the weighing scales, so I am unable to say it." This man was a merchant who used to weigh his merchandise and then sell it to people. But he used to do something seemingly very simple and insignificant: he would remove dust from the scale where he would place the weights, but not remove dust from the scale where he would place the merchandise. In his mind, this would make the merchandise seem a bit heavier, increasing his profit. But what difference would the dust really make?

He had a disease in his heart, which was his desire to take just a little more money from people. He took this lightly, forgetting that the One Who forbade him from taking anything unlawfully is always observing him. **"O believers! Do not devour one another's wealth illegally, but rather trade by mutual consent. And do not kill each other. Surely Allah is ever Merciful to you. And whoever does these things out of hostility and injustice, We shall make him suffer the Fire—and that is easy for Allah."** [Quran 4:29–30]

This man was prevented from saying the Statement of Truth because of this disease in his heart. It seems that over time, this small action darkened his heart, creating a barrier between him and the Statement of Truth at the time of death. If this is how serious this mistake is, then what about even greater errors?

It has been narrated Jesus the son of Maryam ﷺ once brought a dead man back to life. When he was resurrected, the man asked, "Is today the Day of Resurrection?" He was told that it was not, but that Jesus prayed to Allah ﷻ to bring you back to life. The man asked, "O Jesus, why did you bring me back to life?" He replied, "To take a lesson from you. How long has it been since you died?" The man said, "Seventy years." Jesus ﷺ asked, "What did you discover?" He replied, "Allah accepted my righteous actions and overlooked my mistakes—except for one. I once was carrying firewood for some people. When I reached the place where I was to drop it off, I noticed something stuck between my teeth. I took a splinter from the wood, cleaned my teeth with it, and then tossed it away. I was taken to account for this and asked, 'How could you take this splinter from wood that belonged to someone else?' So, for seventy years I have been suspended and rebuked, and will remain so until the owner of the firewood dies, at which point he can pardon me or take his right from me."

This shows what Allah indicates in His Words, **"We will set up the scales of justice on the Day of Resurrection, so no soul will be wronged in the least. And even if a deed is the weight of a mustard seed, We will bring it forth. And sufficient are We as a Reckoner."** [Quran 21:47] And the Prophet ﷺ said, *"When someone seizes what belongs to another Muslim by swearing a false oath, Allah guarantees him the Fire and forbids him from Paradise."* A man asked, "Even if it is a small thing, O Messenger of Allah?" He replied, *"Even if it was just a twig of Ārāk wood."*[46]

He also said ﷺ, *"Whoever wrongfully takes even a handspan of land, the seven earths become clasped to his neck."*[47] This means that if someone

46 Narrated by Muslim in *Kitāb al-Imān* (Hadith 137).

47 Narrated by Bukhārī in *Kitāb Bad' al-Khalq* (Hadith 2023) and Muslim in *Kitāb al-Musāqā* (Hadith 1612).

takes even one handspan of another person's land, it will be tied to his neck on the Day of Resurrection, and he will have to bear the weight of the seven earths—**"and those burdened with wrongdoing will be in loss."** [Quran 20:111] The Prophet ﷺ also said, *"A servant will not become one of the pious until he abandons something harmless out of caution that it might lead to something harmful."*[48]

We find examples in this Ummah's history (and in the previous Prophetic communities) of people who were scrupulous in both scarcity and abundance, out of fear of the Most High ﷻ. Our master 'Umar ibn al-Khaṭṭāb ؓ said, "We used to avoid ninth-tenths of the permissible out of fear that we might fall into something forbidden."[49] This shows the danger of taking what belongs to others and the necessity of caution.

What value is a small feeling of pleasure in a passing moment if it leads to being abased before Allah the Overpowering when He asks you about taking someone else's property! For Him to rebuke you would be painful enough, what then of punishment and having your good deeds taken away?

The Prophet ﷺ described the bankrupt person as someone who acts unjustly, transgresses boundaries, and does not fulfill the rights of others. His good deeds—which initially were as large as mountains—are all lost. His fasting, charity, Prayer, and other righteous deeds are all swept away. The Prophet ﷺ said, *"Do you know who the bankrupt person is?"* The Companions said, "Our understanding of a bankrupt person is someone who has neither money nor property." He then said, *"The bankrupt person from my Ummah is someone who comes on the Day of Resurrection with Prayer, fasting, and zakāt; but he insulted this person, slandered that person, took another person's money, shed someone's blood, and struck yet another*

48 Narrated by al-Tirmidhī (Hadith 2568), Ibn Māja in *Kitāb al-Zuhd* (Hadith 4215), and al-Ḥākim in *al-Mustadrak* who narrated it from 'Aṭṭīya al-Sa'dī and stated that its chain is authentic (*Ṣaḥīḥ*).

49 Narrated by 'Abd al-Razzāq in his *Muṣannaf.*

person. Each one then takes from his good deeds. If his good deeds run out before he gives them what he owes them, he then takes from their wrongs, which are thrown on to him. Then he is hurled into the Fire."[50] His tongue and hands engaged in what Allah ﷻ forbade, so the people he wronged take from his good deeds. If no good deeds remain and he still owes them, he takes the burden of some of their sins. He is then commanded to be taken to the Fire—and we seek refuge in Allah ﷻ.

Being mindful of the rights of others shows the integrity of a person's faith. As one scholar said with respect to this:

> Do not be deluded by a man's patched garments,
> Or his lower garment raised halfway above his calf,
> Instead, show him a gold coin and you will know,
> His scruples or his treachery

A person's true nature becomes clear when dealing with wealth. His withholding, giving, and financial dealings show his faith, scruples, and mindfulness of Allah ﷻ, or the lack thereof.

'Umar ibn al-Khaṭṭāb ؓ said to someone who wanted to vouch for the integrity of a man who was going to testify in court, "Have you ever had financial dealings with him, so that you were able to assess his scrupulousness?" The man said, "No." 'Umar then asked, "Did you ever accompany him on a journey, so that you came to know his character?" Again, he said, "No." 'Umar finally asked, "Were you ever neighbors, so that you came to know of his comings and goings?" The man said, "No." Then 'Umar exclaimed to the man, "Perhaps you saw him standing in Prayer at the mosque, raising and bowing his head?" The man said, "Yes!" 'Umar ؓ then said to him, "Go on your way, for you do not know him."

Outward acts of worship are not sufficient criteria to gauge a person's trueness with Allah ﷻ, nor do they show the firmness of faith in one's

50 Narrated by Muslim in *Kitāb al-Birr wa'l Ṣila wa'l Ādāb* (Hadith 2581).

heart. 'Umar identified three criteria for this purpose: the first is the way one deals with money, the second is traveling with someone, and the third is being someone's neighbor.

SCRUPULOUSNESS IS A MEANS TO ATTAIN ALLAH'S GOOD PLEASURE

Refraining from taking what is forbidden is an immense act, a means for salvation in the Hereafter, and an expansive door to Allah's good pleasure. Therefore, it is necessary to stop one's hands from taking what is unlawful, no matter how insignificant that thing might be. It has been narrated, *"O Mu'ādh, a servant will certainly be asked on the Day of Resurrection about everything, even about the kohl for his eyes and the remnants of clay on his fingers."*[51] Ibn 'Umar would call out to the people, "If you prayed until you became hunched over and fasted until your bodies became like twigs, your actions would only be accepted from you through extensive scrupulousness." In another narration, *"O Abū Hurayra, be scrupulous and you will be the most devout of people."*[52]

The *reality* of worship, which makes you the most devout of people, is attained by being scrupulous. This is how the true faith is established, and societies become purified and stable. People refrain from what Allah has made forbidden according to their varying degrees of faith. The more a person is conscious of this matter, the more virtuous he becomes.

It is mentioned about a righteous family of this Ummah that whenever the husband would go out to earn a living for them, the lady of the house would say to him, "Be mindful of Allah with regards to what your hands acquire and what you bring into our home for us to eat. We can endure hunger, thirst, and lack of clothing—but we cannot endure the

51 Narrated by Ibn Ḥātim in his Tafsīr and Abū Nu'aym narrated the likes of it in *al-Ḥilya*.

52 Narrated by Ibn Māja in *Kitāb al-Zuhd* (Hadith 4217).

Fire. So, if you bring anything into our home that is dubious or forbidden, you are the one who will be held accountable for it. We have fulfilled our responsibility before Allah." This was the counsel that righteous women gave righteous men, and this was the state of families who had faith.

Compare this to the lower self that loves to take whatever comes its way without any care for where it came from. Alternatively, people who deem their son or husband as virtuous, generous, and intelligent when he brings them wealth by any means. Whoever is indifferent to the way his provision comes to him, Allah has no concern for which valley of Hellfire He casts him into.

O Allah, grant us scrupulousness and enable us to refrain from all that is unlawful. Make us vigilant of You in all that we take and give, and take care of us in a way befitting of You in all our affairs, inward and outward—O Most Merciful. May Allah's peace and blessings be upon the Chosen One, Muhammad, and upon his Family and Companions. And all praise belongs to Allah, Lord of the Worlds.

CHAPTER 12

Striking with the Hand

All praise belongs to Allah, the All-Knowing, All-Aware. We bear witness that He is Allah, there is no god except Him, One without partner. To Him belongs the dominion and to Him belongs all praise. He possesses all good and has power over all things. We also bear witness that our Prophet and coolness of our eyes, our master Muhammad, is His Servant and Messenger. He sent him with guidance and the religion of truth to make it prevail over all other religions, even though the polytheists hate this. O Allah, send Your blessings endlessly upon Your Chosen One, our master Muhammad, and upon his purified Family, noble Companions, and all who follow their path in public and in secret.

To proceed: The pure Sharia guides us on how to use our hands, forbidding us from using them to harm or violate the rights of others. It outlines specific situations where our hands may be used to strike. Even in these situations, this must be done in a specified manner when it is beneficial to do so, such as when disciplining, correcting, and promoting good and repelling evil. We have been given this system to elevate us from only causing harm and conflict.

When Allah ﷻ judges people, He takes into account the impact of every hand that struck or caused harm to another. It has come in narration that Allah ﷻ says,

> I am the Sovereign. I am the Judge. It is not fitting for anyone from the people of Paradise to enter Paradise while they owe someone from the people of the Fire reparations for a wrong; nor for anyone from the people of the Fire to enter to the Fire while they owe someone from the people of Paradise reparations for a wrong—even a slap.[53]

On the Day of Resurrection, it is not just humans who will seek retribution. The Prophet ﷺ said, *"All rights will be restored on the Day of Resurrection until even the hornless sheep takes what it is owed from the horned one."*[54] The horned sheep will have its horns taken and given to the hornless one and then it will strike the other to the same extent to which it was struck in this world. If this is the extent of Allah's justice between animals, how will His justice be between those who are morally accountable? There are people who possess hearing, sight, and intellects who have received the message, yet still remain neglectful of the rights of others. We know that our master Muhammad ﷺ never struck a woman or child. He only ever struck a man during battle when struggling in the way of Allah ﷻ.

THE BOUNDARIES OF HITTING

The striking permitted in the Sacred Law is intended solely for disciplinary purposes. The objective is the rectification and refinement of the self, not inflicting harm or pain. Such discipline is used as a means for someone when learning, or by a father with his son, or by a ruler with someone under his governance. In each instance, it should be done in a way that does not transgress the bounds. For example, it is forbidden to strike the face and to shed blood.

The Sacred Law also legislates certain physical punishments for specific transgressions such as drinking alcohol or fornication. These are

53 Narrated by Aḥmad with a sound (*ḥasan*) chain, and by al-Ṭabarānī in *al-Kabīr*.
54 Narrated by Muslim in *Kitāb al-Birr wa'l Ṣila wa'l Ādāb* (Hadith 2582).

clearly defined in the Quran and Sunna, aiming to deter people from falling into lowly acts that displease Allah ﷻ and cause them to miss out on great good in this life and the next. The Prophet ﷺ said, *"When someone commits adultery or drinks wine, Allah removes faith from him just like a person removes a garment of clothing off of his head."*[55]

The Prophet ﷺ saw Abū Masʿūd al-Anṣārī in a state of anger, beating his slave, so he called out to him from behind, *"Abū Masʿūd, be sure that Allah has more power over you than you have over him."* He turned around and saw that it was the Messenger of Allah ﷺ who had spoken. Abū Masʿūd said, "O Messenger of Allah, I set him free for the sake of Allah." The Messenger of Allah ﷺ responded, saying, *"Had you not done so, you would have been scorched by the Fire."*[56]

This teaches us the limit and method of hitting, emphasizing that exceeding these boundaries will result in retribution on the Day of Judgment. A person cannot be deluded by his strength and ability to harm others. The power of our hands must only be employed for defending the religion, all that is good, and what truly benefits people. We may use our hands to resist an oppressive aggressor to stop him from his wrongdoing, or someone who is antagonistic towards Allah ﷻ and His Messenger ﷺ and is harmful, belligerent, and tyrannical towards people. It is right to use our strength to prevent oppression and wrongdoing. Using it for a purpose other than this only brings a person shame and loss.

THE DANGER OF KILLING

Knowing this makes us careful of the way we use our hands, which could potentially lead to the terrible act of shedding someone's blood. The most destructive sin after associating partners with Allah ﷻ (*shirk*) is

55 Narrated by al-Ḥākim in *al-Mustadrak* with an authentic chain on the authority of Abū Hurayra.

56 Narrated by Muslim in *Kitāb al-Īmān* (Hadith 1659).

unlawfully taking another's life, which was made inviolable by Allah. This is so grave that the Messenger of Allah ﷺ said, *"If two Muslims confront each other with their swords, then both the killer and the one killed will enter the Fire."* He was then asked, "We understand that with regards to the killer, but why the one who was killed?" The Prophet replied, *"He wanted to kill the other."*[57] He died while intending to kill the other, so he is in the Fire—we seek refuge in Allah ﷻ.

Allah ﷻ said, **"And whoever kills a believer intentionally, his reward is Hell—where he will stay forever. Allah is angry with him, condemns him, and has prepared a tremendous punishment for him."** [Quran 4:93] Contemplate these words and reflect on the One who is saying them, and this will suffice you from being forcibly rebuked about this abominable act. The Prophet ﷺ also said, *"A believer is safely within the bounds of his religion as long as he does not shed blood unlawfully."*[58] If he sheds inviolable blood, he has limited his own chances—and Allah's refuge is sought.

A Muslim must therefore be extremely careful of striking another person. It is not permissible to hit anyone or cause them pain (except in the situations mentioned previously). When one is careful in this way, the hand becomes a source of benefit instead of harm. When giving something good or when disciplining, the hand's action benefits in either case, because the action is connected to the righteous intention of rectifying oneself and society. This is on the condition that one is scrupulous when doing so, which then prevents him from an even more severe act, which is the epitome of sin: unlawfully shedding the blood of a believer.

Scholars differ on whether the repentance of one who kills another Muslim will even be accepted or not. This is despite the fact that repentance is accepted for all sins, even the most abominable, such as associ-

57 Narrated by al-Bukhārī in *Kitāb al-Fitan* (Hadith 6672) and Muslim in *Kitāb al-Fitan* (Hadith 2888).

58 Narrated by al-Bukhārī in *Kitāb al-Dīyāt* (Hadith 6496).

ating partners with Allah (*shirk*). Scholars agree that repentance from *shirk* by way of *tawḥīd* and believing in Allah ﷻ is accepted, yet they differ over whether the repentance of one who deliberately kills another Muslim is accepted or not. This shows how severe this terrible crime is.

It is an obligation to remain within the boundaries and satisfy the conditions of the Sacred Law with regards to the hand's actions, which will be held to account soon enough. **"The Day when every soul will be presented with whatever good it has done. And it will wish that its misdeeds were far, far away. And Allah warns you about Himself. And Allah is Ever Gracious to His servants."** [Quran 3:30]

O Allah, protect our hands from all that brings humiliation, disgrace, and an evil outcome. End our lives in a way befitting of Your grace, O Living, Self-Subsistent. Purify our limbs and hearts and turn to us in mercy so that we may turn back to You. Grant us this by the eminence of Your Prophet Muhammad, may Your abundant peace and blessings be upon him, his Family, Companions, and all who follow his Way. All praise belongs to Allah, Lord of the Worlds.

CHAPTER 13

Watching What We Eat

All praise belongs to Allah, the Powerful, the Invincible. May Allah's peace and blessings be upon His Servant, the Chosen One, the Trustworthy, our master Muhammad, and upon his Family, Companions, and those who follow them with excellence until the Day of Judgment.

To proceed: Another thing we use our hands for is consuming food and drink. What our stomachs absorb has both an outward and inward impact. It affects the body, soul, and heart. This is why the Sacred Law, in its perfection, gave us rulings and etiquettes related to food and drink. These rulings and etiquettes protect us from eating things that are dubious or forbidden. When we observe these etiquettes and principles, we receive the downpour of Allah's mercy. Allah ﷻ said, **"Eat of the lawful and good things provided to you by Allah."** [Quran 5:88] He ﷻ also said, **"O believers! Eat from the good things We have provided for you. And give thanks to Allah if you truly worship Him."** [Quran 2:172] And the Prophet ﷺ said, *"Allah is pleased with a servant when he eats food and praises Allah for it, or when he drinks and praises Allah for it."*[59]

59 Narrated by Muslim in *Kitāb al-Dhikr wa'l Du'ā* (Hadith 2734).

LAWFUL FOOD & DRINK

The first consideration with respect to food or drink is that it be lawful. When Muslims are not mindful that Allah is observing them, it is easy for them to consume what is unlawful. This causes them to be dishonest and to transgress against others.

Although both believers and non-believers share in the understanding that violating the rights of others leads to chaos and disorder in society, the believer is distinguished by knowing that it damages his future and ultimate end. It subjects him to Allah's wrath سبحانه وتعالى, Who will then hold him accountable for what he has done.

Imam 'Abd-Allah ibn al-Mubārak said, "Refusing one *dirham* from a dubious source is preferable to me than giving 600,000 *dirhams* in charity." Refusing that one dubious *dirham* is proof of true faith and fear of the All-Merciful سبحانه وتعالى.

Imam Abū Ḥanīfa رضي الله عنه was so scrupulous that he would refuse even a large amount of money if there was the slightest doubt that it was not entirely lawful. He once sent a shipment of clothing to be sold by his broker. In the shipment there was one item of clothing that had a defect. Imam Abū Ḥanīfa informed the broker about this item and instructed him to not sell the clothing until he had shown the defect to the buyer. His broker found a buyer who was willing to purchase the entire shipment, but he forgot to inform the buyer of the defective item.

When his broker sent a letter to Imam Abū Ḥanīfa informing him that he had sold the shipment of clothing at a good price and had made a large profit, Imam Abū Ḥanīfa asked him, "Did you show the buyer the defective item?" He responded that he had forgotten to do so because the buyer had bought the entire shipment wholesale. Imam Abū Ḥanīfa wrote back to him, "Do not take any money from this sale—neither the profit nor the capital. Set it aside and give it away in charity, and do not corrupt my trade with any money from it." He would not even take back his capital because it had mixed with profit made from the defective item that had not been disclosed, thereby deceiving a Muslim. The Messenger of Allah ﷺ said, *"Whoever deceives us is not of us."*[60] Imam Abū Ḥanīfa refrained from taking that money out of fear of Allah ﷻ.

One of the main purposes of wealth is to buy food, which enters the stomach, is ingested, and then cultivates a person's physique and strength. As the Hadith states, *"All flesh that grows from forbidden food belongs in the Fire."*[61] There are numerous etiquettes related to eating, including sitting in a particular way, remembering Allah's Name ﷻ at the onset, and saying *"al-ḥamdu lillāh"* when finishing the meal. These etiquettes reinforce the importance of being careful of what we eat and teach us to investigate whether the food is permissible or forbidden. True faith is only established by scrupulously avoiding the unlawful.

The lives of the noble Companions and those who followed them with excellence exemplify what it means to be cautious in our dealings. Dhu'l Nūn al-Miṣrī embodied this virtue when someone sent food to him while he was in prison. He apologized to the person who sent it, saying, "I know that your wealth is lawful, because you are scrupulous, but this food brought to me on the tray of someone who is a wrongdoer," meaning the prison guard. "I cannot eat food that came to me from such a person." This is, without a doubt, beyond what is obligatory. However, it illustrates a high degree of scrupulousness, which is befitting of the Entirely True (*Ṣiddiqūn*) and those possessed with refined souls, who are the best of people.

Abū Bakr al-Ṣiddīq ؓ had a servant who traded on his behalf. Each day the boy would bring some of what he earned to Abū Bakr and keep whatever remained. Abū Bakr would use his earnings to buy food. One

---

60 Narrated by Muslim in *Kitāb al-Imān* (Hadith 143).

61 Narrated by al-Bayhaqī in *Shuʿab al-Imān* from the Hadith of Kaʿb ibn ʿUjra. It is also narrated by al-Tirmidhī who declared it sound (*ḥasan*) with the following wording: *"Any flesh that grows from forbidden 'food', then the Fire has more right to it."*

day, he brought some food and because Abū Bakr ﷺ was hungry and busy with a task, he immediately accepted the food and ate it. The servant said to him, "Before you eat, you usually ask me, 'Where did you get this food from?' Usually, you are reserved and don't eat it until you verify its source. But today you didn't ask me!" He replied, "I was busy and forgot to ask. Where did you get this food from?" The boy said, "I passed by such-and-such family, and they were having a wedding celebration. They gave me some food because they remembered me from the Days of Ignorance when I would pretend to be a fortuneteller and predict their future for them." When the servant said this, Abū Bakr immediately reacted scrupulously.

Those people would have given the boy (or anyone else) food anyway because they were celebrating a wedding, and the Arab custom is to give generously to anyone who attends their wedding. But Abū Bakr ﷺ said, "They gave you food because they knew you from your fortunetelling days! This is dubious food that has entered my stomach." He then placed his finger in his mouth and forced himself to vomit, which made a loud sound. Some neighbors came by and asked, "What's wrong with the Messenger of Allah's Caliph?" He replied, "Some dubious food entered my stomach that I must remove." After forcing the food out, he continued to seek Allah's forgiveness for whatever effects remained in his stomach. His neighbors said to him, "You almost killed yourself to get the food out!" He said, "I heard the Prophet say, *'All flesh that grows from forbidden food belongs in the Fire.'* I feared that this food would add to my flesh, making it deserving of the Fire. If my soul had to leave my body to get the food out, I would have done so." May Allah be well pleased with him![62]

62 The beginning of this story is narrated by al-Bukhārī in *Kitāb Faḍā'il al-Ṣaḥāba* (Hadith 3920).

A WARNING AGAINST DISREGARDING SCRUPULOUSNESS

These examples emphasize the impact of the Messenger of Allah's method of educating ﷺ. We cannot turn away from his teachings by preferring what is being presented to us today and made to appear appealing. If we do so, we become blind followers of anyone who comes along, and we lose the foundational principles of our religion. Muslims must awaken to the reality that after today there is another Day, after this life there is a judgment, and that we attain all benefit through scrupulousness. The Hadith states, *"When someone leaves something for Allah's sake, Allah will compensate him with something better than it."*[63] Pursuing things without caution and scrupulousness has terrible consequences. Muslims will be afflicted with the same things that afflict those who do not believe in Allah ﷻ. Their reckoning is even more intense because they betrayed their covenant after professing the Two Testimonies of Faith and taking on the weighty oath. We must be careful of what enters our stomachs and the stomachs of our spouses, children, and household, and ensure that it comes from a lawful income.

People might say, "What can we do? Dubious and forbidden things are widespread, as is usury!" We say to them: the command to be scrupulous still stands, despite dubious things being widespread in this day and age. There is a big difference between someone who does not care and someone who does, and between someone who pursues dubious things without any concern and someone who is careful to the extent of his ability.

Some matters are completely forbidden, while others are gray areas. Some are very murky while others are only a little. The way to differentiate between these things is by gaining an understanding of the Sharia. "If the

63 Narrated by Aḥmad with the wording: *"Whenever you leave something for Allah's sake, Mighty and Majestic, Allah will replace it for you with something that is better for you."* Al-Bayhaqī in *al-Sunan al-Kubrā* narrates it with the wording: *"Whenever you leave something out of being conscious of Allah, Allah will replace it for you with something better than it."*

world was filled with blood, Allah would still grant the believer a lawful sustenance."[64] We must then, to the extent of our ability, avoid those things that are completely forbidden and highly dubious. We should choose things that are furthest from doubt, according to our ability. And Allah ﷻ will guide the one who seeks good and grant him steadfastness.

We ask Allah ﷻ to grant us the understanding that Allah's reward is better and more lasting. We ask that we be granted the ability to overcome our lower selves and make our dealings compliant with the Sacred Law.

O Allah, grant us enabling grace to accomplish this, and spread goodness within us, for us, by us, from us, and upon us. Do not leave us to our own selves, nor to anyone from Your creation, for even the blink of an eye. Do not try us with what You have given us or what You have taken away from us—O Most Merciful! May Allah's peace and blessings be upon the Chosen One, Muhammad, and upon his Family, Companions, and all those who follow his way. All praise belongs to Allah, Lord of the Worlds.

---

64 Quoted by Imam al-Ghazālī in the *Iḥyā'*, attributed to Sahl ibn 'Abd-Allāh al-Tustarī. Translator's note: This means that even in the most unlikely circumstances, whenever a person is mindful of Allah, He ﷻ will provide for them. As Allah ﷻ says, **"Whoever is mindful of Allah, He will make a way out for him and provide for him from sources he could never imagine."** [Quran 65:2–3]

CHAPTER 14

Raising Our Hands to Ask Allah ﷻ

All praise belongs to Allah, the most complete and perfect praise, in every state. May Allah's peace and blessings be upon His Servant who guides, Muhammad ibn 'Abd-Allah, and upon his Family, Companions, and all who follow his guidance.

To proceed: In previous chapters, we discussed various ways we can use our hands. Some are means to attain benefit, success, and felicity, and some are the opposite.

One of the principles that the Sacred Law teaches us is to be wary of constantly holding our hands out to seek material things from other people. We should never be greedy and pester others. We maintain our dignity by asking our Lord ﷻ to fulfill our needs. This does not mean, however, that we are too proud to ask others when we are genuinely in need or when asking to help other Muslims who are in need.

THE BLAMEWORTHINESS OF ASKING FROM PEOPLE

We have been commanded to earn a lawful livelihood, and there are many ways to do so. We will then have enough for our needs, and we will not have to ask others. The Prophet ﷺ said, *"The upper hand is better than the lower below.*"[65] The upper hand is the giving hand, and the lower hand is the one receiving. Wise people heeded this lesson, and they only held out their hands to the Lord of people. As one of them said,

> Do not ask for a need from the Son of Adam,
> But ask from the One whose doors are never closed
> Allah is angered when you abandon asking Him,
> But the Son of Adam, when you ask him, is angered!

When you persistently request from someone, even if he has given to you once or twice before, he eventually will become annoyed with you, regardless of how generous he is. On the other hand, when you persistently request from the Lord of Creation ﷻ, He increases in good-pleasure, generosity, and beneficence. The Prophet ﷺ said, *"Allah loves those who are persistent in their supplication."*[66] Taking your needs to your Lord is a source of honor, increase, and success for the believer.

Allah ﷻ then facilitates the fulfillment of your supplication at the hands of whomever He wills from His creation. Your heart's attachment to Allah is foundational for your success and prosperity. It protects you from falling into the trap of associating outcomes to people independently, which veils you from witnessing the One ﷻ who facilitated those outcomes.

The giver always profits, regardless of whether the person he gives to is truly deserving or not. The Prophet ﷺ said, *"Someone asking for money has a right, even if he comes riding on a horse."*[67]

If someone knows with certainty that the money he gives will be used for something forbidden, only then is he obligated to refrain from giving. But if he does not know that, then he is rewarded for giving to

65 Narrated by al-Bukhārī in *Kitāb al-Zakāt* (Hadith 1361), and by Muslim in *Kitāb al-Zakāt* (Hadith 1034).

66 Narrated by al-Ṭabarānī and Abū'l Shaykh.

67 Narrated by Abū Dāwūd

that person. The person asking will be held accountable if he lied about his true condition, and it is impermissible for him to use anything that he receives.

It is not permissible for someone to ask from others, claiming poverty or neediness, if they have enough provisions for an entire day and night. Then, if a day and night have passed and he no longer has anything, he can only ask for what he needs for one full day and night. The Prophet ﷺ said, *"A person continues to ask from others until he meets Allah without even a piece of flesh left on his face."*[68] In other words, the flesh on his face falls off in vain because he would regularly extend his hand to other than Allah ﷻ out of greed and desire.

A BELIEVER'S HONOR IS IN ASKING ALLAH

We must honor our hands by raising them to the All-Merciful ﷻ for all our needs and requests, for He is the Self-Sufficient and He is pleased with His servant's request. He gives freely and He loves those who persistently call upon Him in *duʿā*. He said ﷻ, **"Your Lord has proclaimed, 'Call upon Me, I will respond to you. Surely those who are too proud to worship Me will enter Hell, fully humbled.'"** [Quran 40:60]

Whenever one of the people of spiritual realization and refinement had a need from a specific person, he would take his need first to Allah, and ask and turn to Him ﷻ. Afterwards, he would go to that person and tell him of his need, but all the while his heart would remain attached to Allah ﷻ. He would always thank the person who fulfilled his need or excuse him if he did not fulfill it. A wise man once wrote to a person saying, "I have a certain need, so if you fulfill it, then Allah ﷻ is the Fulfiller and He is the One who enabled you to goodness, and I will thank you. If you do not fulfill it, then Allah ﷻ is the One who did not will

68 Narrated by Muslim in *Kitāb al-Zakāt* (Hadith 1040).

it, and you are excused." This understanding rectifies people's dealings and purifies their inner states.

The weaknesses of the lower self, however, make people stubbornly hold to the idea that "This person gave to me," and, "That person didn't give to me," and, "That person is the reason I didn't get anything." They forget that they and all these means are subjugated to the power of the All-Powerful and the dominance of the Dominator. When a person gives, in reality, it is because Allah ﷻ made him give. If he withholds, it is because Allah has made him withhold. With that being said, a person is rewarded for giving and reprimanded for withholding when he is able to spend in the way of goodness.

When people's hearts are attached to creation and forget the Creator, this burdens them and causes various sicknesses such as enmity and hatred. People often deceive others, cheat, and lie in order to attain wealth and the things of the world. Those who do this lose in both this life and the Hereafter. As the years pass, they experience the outcome of what they used to think was good, and the world is filled with examples of this. Many people become exposed in this world before the next. And in the next life, the affair is far more serious, **"The Day all will appear ˹before Allah˺ and nothing about them will be hidden from Him. ˹He will ask,˺ 'Who does all authority belong to this Day?' To Allah—the One, the Dominator!"** [Quran 40:16]

WITNESSING ALLAH AS THE GIVER

Anyone with faith must firstly express his needs to the All-Merciful ﷻ. If he needs to speak to anyone, he should do so after his heart resigns to the fact that the affair belongs to Allah ﷻ. He should then seek out the person with the understanding that Allah has only made that person a means. If that person fulfills his need, he should not allow his heart to become completely attached to that person, thereby forgetting Allah's blessing. If that person does not fulfill his need, he should not hold a grudge against him. He should not think, 'He withheld from me.' That is the thinking of someone who does not rely on a higher power or who thinks that Allah's Will ﷻ does not apply to what he does or does not receive.

On this point, Imam al-Ḥaddād said,

> What is apportioned to you will surely come,
> And what is for another will not reach you,
> So busy yourself with your Lord and your duties:
> The obligation of realization and the Sacred Law
> You and all creation are servants,
> And Allah does with us whatever He wills
> Worry and distress, they're of no benefit
> The divine decree precedes all, so be still
> Abandon your worries—whatever is decreed will happen

This is how a person's state with Allah ﷻ and with creation is elevated: by witnessing that the true Giver and Withholder is Allah ﷻ. No one can withhold something from you if Allah wills for it to reach you, and no one can give you something if Allah prevents it. Allah ﷻ said, **"Whatever mercy Allah opens up for people, none can withhold it. And whatever He withholds, none but Him can release it."** [Quran 35:2] He also tells us ﷻ, **"And Allah has favored some of you over others in provision. But those who have been much favored would not share their wealth with those bondspeople in their possession, making them their equals. Do they then deny Allah's favors?"** [Quran 16:71]

It was agreed that Muʿāwiya ibn Abū Sufyan would send Ḥasan ibn ʿAlī ؓ a stipend every year. Imam Ḥasan would spend it on his many guests and give large sums in charity. One year, the stipend did not arrive as usual. His debts started to mount up and he was in a difficult situation. He decided to send a letter to remind Muʿāwiya of the agreement and he asked for a pen and ink so that he could write to him. Then he decided against writing the letter.

That night, he had a vision of his grandfather, the Chosen One ﷺ. The Prophet said to him, *"My son, you called for a pen and inkwell so that you could write to someone who, just like you, is created?"* He replied, "I was going to do that, O Messenger of Allah. Then I stopped." The Prophet ﷺ then said, *"Do not do that."* Ḥasan رضي الله عنه asked, "What then should I do?" He said, *"Say: 'O Allah, cast into my heart hope in You and cut off any hope I have in other than You, so that I have hope only in You. O Allah, however weak I am, however deficient my actions are, however short my desire for good falls, and although I have not asked You, and my tongue has not pronounced such a request, I ask You for the certainty that You have given any one of Your servants from the first to the last of them. So bless me with it, O Most Merciful!* Imam Ḥasan said, "I persistently called upon Allah with this supplication, and less than a week later, he sent far more than he would normally send me. I then saw the Messenger of Allah ﷺ and informed him. He said to me, *'My son, this is the result when someone places his hope in the Creator and not in creation.'*"[69] Aspirations must be connected to Allah and good should be sought from Him سبحانه وتعالى.

Hishām ibn 'Abd al-Malik, who was a ruler at the time, entered the Ka'ba and saw Sālim ibn 'Abd-Allāh ibn 'Umar ibn al-Khaṭṭāb. Hishām said to him, "Ask me for whatever you need." He replied, "I feel shame before Allah to ask from anyone other than Him while I am in His House." When they both came out of the Mosque, Hishām said, "Now that you are outside of Allah's House, ask me for whatever you need." Sālim said to him, "Worldly needs or needs of the Hereafter?" He replied, "Worldly needs." To which Sālim said, "By Allah, I did not ask for the world from the One who owns it, so how can I ask for it from someone who does not own it?"[70]

69 Narrated by Ibn 'Asākir.

70 Narrated by Ibn 'Asākir and al-Dhahabī in *Siyar A'lām al-Nubalā'.*

We turn to Allah ﷻ, asking Him to attach our hearts to Him and hold our hands back from anything unbefitting. We ask Him ﷻ to cast the hope in Him into our hearts and that He cuts off our hope in anything other than Him—He is the Most Generous of all. May peace and blessings of Allah be upon the Chosen One, Muhammad, and upon his Family and Companions. All praise belongs to Allah, Lord of the Worlds.

CHAPTER 15

Protecting Our Homes

All praise belongs to Allah, the Sovereign, the Magnanimous, the Most Generous. May Allah's peace and blessings be upon His Servant, the kind and merciful,[71] our master Muhammad and upon his Family, Companions, and all those who follow his honorable way and Straight Path.

To proceed: Consuming doubtful things and allowing them to enter our bodies has an extremely harmful impact on our lives, both in this life and the Hereafter. Guarding the stomach from consuming doubtful things is a sign of belief in Allah ﷻ and His Messenger ﷺ. It is a means for salvation, protects the body and soul, and ensures well-being in this world and the next. The priority is to avoid consuming things that are forbidden: such as what has been stolen or wrongly taken; those that are intrinsically forbidden, such as carrion, pork, and alcohol; as well as those that are forbidden due to an incidental cause, such as food acquired through an unlawful income.

When we avoid these things, we are then able to appreciate Allah's wisdom in making these things forbidden and understand how He saves

71 Translator's note: This refers to the titles given to the blessed Prophet ﷺ by Allah ﷻ in the Quran, **"There has certainly come to you a Messenger from among yourselves. Your suffering distresses him. He is deeply concerned 'for your well-being' and he is full of kindness and mercy towards the believers."** [Quran 9:128]

us from damnation and evil. So, we must conscientiously select what food and drink we allow to enter our stomachs and adhere to this standard with our families and those under our care.

The Sacred Law warns against stealing, which has a severe legal punishment due to its extreme harm and danger. Allah ﷻ said, **"Cut off the hands of thieves, whether they are man or woman, as a punishment for what they have done—a deterrent from Allah. And Allah is Almighty, All-Wise."** [Quran 5:38] A scholar was once asked about someone who cuts off another person's hand—what restitution could the victim demand? He said, "Five hundred *dinārs*." He was then asked, "If a person steals a quarter of a *dinār*, would his hand be cut off?" He said, "Yes." He was then asked, "How could a hand be cut off for stealing a quarter of a *dinār*, but the restitution given to someone ⌜who lost a hand⌝ is five hundred *dinārs*?!" The scholar replied, "It is only cut off because of its treachery. But if someone wrongfully cuts another person's hand off, the restitution he is owed is five hundred *dinārs*." Al-Muʿarrī explains this in poetic form,

> Five hundred gold coins are a hand's restitution,
> But cut off for a quarter—what's the reason?

Al-Qāḍī ʿAbd al-Wahhāb replied with,

> The honor of trustworthiness made it precious,
> And treachery's lowliness devalued it—understand the Creator's wisdom!

Ibn al-Jawzī, replied when asked about this, "When it was reliable, it was valuable; but when it betrayed, it became disgraced."

It has come in a Hadith, *"Allah curses the thief. He steals an egg, so his hand is cut off; and he steals a rope, so his hand is cut off."*[72] Scholars say

72 Narrated by al-Bukhārī in *Kitāb al-Ḥudūd* (Hadith 6401), and by Muslim in *Kitāb al-Ḥudūd* (Hadith 1687).

that this means that he starts with stealing an egg, then on to more and more valuable things, which eventually leads him to stealing something worth a quarter of a *dinār*, which at that point would result in his hand getting cut off.

AVOIDING THE FORBIDDEN IS ESSENTIAL FOR SALVATION

Shunning forbidden things is essential for safety and salvation. When families become firmly rooted in these meanings, they are protected from what causes wretchedness in both abodes. Let us then be careful in guarding our stomachs from anything forbidden. Anything that removes the intellect or deadens the heart's feelings is considered an intoxicant and is forbidden. The Messenger of Allah ﷺ said, *"Every intoxicant is* khamr, *and all* khamr *is forbidden."*[73]

Consuming intoxicants causes people's faith to be stripped from their hearts. This act only becomes widespread when people's awareness of Allah ﷻ, the realities of faith, spiritual cultivation, mutual counsel to truth and patience, and the connection to the divine law have been lost. Our sons and daughters are often exposed to intoxicants when their parents are absent. This occurs when parents are neglectful of warning their children and developing their awareness, which is done by teaching them that a person cannot attain honor by following the desires of the lower self. Rather, a person must judge doubtful things according to the criteria of the Sacred Law to determine whether it is permissible or forbidden. A Muslim must know that consuming forbidden things only results in shame, sickness, punishment, and other difficulties. This motivates him to resist the passions of the lower self in consuming those forbidden things.

Unfortunately, due to the neglect of some parents, their children have

73 Narrated by Muslim in *al-Ashriba* (Hadith 2001), and by al-Tirmidhī, Ibn Māja, and al-Nasāʾī.

fallen into this. This might be from the influence of what they see on television or online. In some cases, they start taking drugs because their parents are users. These parents bring ruin upon themselves and their own children by consuming substances that strip away the faith of whoever uses them. The Prophet ﷺ said, *"An adulterer, while he is committing adultery, is not a believer; and a person, while drinking an intoxicant, is not a believer."*[74] So in the moment he consumes the intoxicant, he has no faith whatsoever—actually, at that moment, faith is wrenched from his heart and might never return.

THE IMPORTANCE OF GUARDING OUR HOMES

Families need to instill true Islamic principles within their children so that they do not become susceptible to disobeying Allah with their stomachs and hands by consuming intoxicants or other forbidden things. In fact, we should aspire to protect them from even consuming *doubtful* things and things that scholars differ on. This is what we were taught by the Messenger of Allah ﷺ, when he said, *"The lawful is clear, and the forbidden is clear, and between the two are doubtful matters that are unknown to most people. Whoever avoids what is doubtful will save his religion and honor. But whoever indulges in them will indulge in the forbidden. It is like a shepherd who allows his flock to graze too close to a sanctuary, all but grazing in it. Every king has a sanctuary, and Allah's sanctuary is His prohibitions."*[75]

We must be extremely vigilant of what enters the stomach of anyone we are responsible for feeding. We must protect them by closing the doors that lead them to even think about consuming forbidden things. These doors may be the company they keep, the content they watch, or

74 Narrated by al-Bukhārī in *Kitāb al-Ḥudūd* (Hadith 6390), and by Muslim in *Kitāb al-Īmān* (Hadith 57).

75 Narrated by al-Bukhārī in *Kitāb al-Imān* (Hadith 52), and by Muslim in *al-Musāqā* (Hadith 1599).

the material they read. Temptations assail them from many angles and the opportunities to engage in forbidden things are abundant.

With that being said, everyone agrees that social media can be used for good, but few people use it for that purpose. We must revive our resolve to control our devices and not let them control us. We must use them and not let them use us. Most people are controlled by these devices and not the other way around. They take the most valuable things away from people: their values, manners, religion, family, and role models. And what have people really gained from them?

Society's problems are not solved by what people watch on their screens. Rather, solutions are found in the striving of sincere and truthful people, by listening to Allah ﷻ and His Messenger ﷺ, and through beneficial knowledge. Notice how people have been deluded into thinking that television shows, often conveying evil things to us, teach us how to solve our problems. In reality, they create more problems for us. We need to show strong resolve in order for us and our families to benefit from these devices and not to be harmed by them. This is an immense responsibility that stems from understanding what truly benefits. We must work hard to raise our children so that they willingly and confidently accept guidance from us.

We must be meticulous in supervising what our sons and daughters consume, ensuring that they avoid harmful substances. We must take special care to avoid things that are doubtful and check the ingredients of the food we eat as they may contain pork products or other forbidden things. We have to be aware that this is about more than just eating chocolate or enjoying a drink without any consideration for what ingredients are added. One's duty to Allah ﷻ takes precedence over his wants and desires.

We ask Allah to take us by the hand to what benefits us inwardly and outwardly, and we ask Him to cast into our hearts the hope in Him alone—He is the Most Generous of all. May Allah's peace and blessings be upon the Chosen One Muhammad, and his Family and Companions. All praise belongs to Allah, Lord of the Worlds.

CHAPTER 16

Debating

All praise belongs to Allah, Lord of the Worlds, the Sovereign, the Most Generous. May Allah's peace and blessings be upon the one sent as a mercy to all the worlds, His Beloved, Muhammad, the best of servants—and upon his pure Family, noble Companions, and all who follow their path until the Day we stand before the Most-Forgiving Sovereign.

To proceed: One of the most important duties in the life of a believer is to speak well. The words that we express with the tongue are the fruits of what is in our hearts. Let us now examine one type of speech: debating. We need to carefully study when debating could be beneficial and bring people together, and when it could have the potential to be damaging and divide people, which is most often the case.

ARGUING & DISPUTING ARE EVILS OF THE TONGUE

One of the tongue's evils that we must avoid is to argue with someone in order to win the argument and humiliate them. Another of the tongue's evils is disputing, which is to continue to defend one's point even after it becomes clear that it is incorrect. When reflecting on divine and prophetic guidance, we see that we should avoid argumentation and disputing. Only in rare instances does it becomes required, such as when clarifying the truth to prevent dissension. Even when disputing becomes necessary, Allah commands us to do so in the best way. He has said ﷻ, **"Do not argue with the People of the Book, unless you do so in the best way."** [Quran 29:46] And He ﷻ says, **"⌜O Prophet,⌝ invite to the Way of your Lord with wisdom and kind advice, and only dispute with them in the best manner."** [Quran 16:125]

How does one dispute in "the best manner?" Undoubtedly, it cannot be vengeful, to belittle others, for sectarian purposes, or other disgraceful motives. One disputes in "the best manner" when he conveys the truth and refutes the arguments of those who are misguided and mislead others. This is the circumstance when we have been commanded to dispute in the best manner. We must refrain from debating in a way that goes beyond this foundational objective, which is to establish proof, clarify evidence, and guide those seeking nearness to Allah ﷻ.

By understanding disputing in this way, we become illuminated by the light of the Prophetic Sunna. How did he ﷺ dispute with the People of the Book, the polytheists, and others? What words did he use? What did his reminders consist of? Did they contain any insults? Did he ever say anything extreme that drove people away? The Prophet ﷺ explicitly said, *"I was not sent as someone who curses others. I was only sent as a mercy."*[76] He also said ﷺ, *"A believer is not someone who insults, curses, or says obscene things."*[77]

How then could a Muslim argue aggressively with his fellow believers and accuse them of the vilest offense—which is disbelief and associating partners with Allah—because of a difference of opinion? This is sectarianism, extremism, and arrogance, and this is the kind of useless disputation that is indicative of being misguided, as mentioned in the

76 Narrated by Muslim in *Kitāb al-Birr wa'l Ṣila wa'l Ādāb* (Hadith 2599).

77 Narrated by al-Tirmidhī in *Al-Birr wa'l Ṣila* (Hadith 2043), Aḥmad in *al-Musnad*, al-Bukhārī in *al-Adab*, Ibn Ḥibbān in his *Ṣaḥīḥ*, and al-Ḥākim in *al-Mustadrak*—on the authority of Ibn Mas'ūd.

Hadith, *"Whenever a people go astray after receiving guidance, they take to disputation."*[78]

The acts of worship that Allah ﷻ has given us teach us to be balanced so that disputing does not change from being done in the "best manner" to being done wrongfully. For example, when we fast, we are told to abstain from disputing, insulting, and arguing. The Prophet ﷺ said, *"On a day when one is fasting, he should not say anything obscene nor shout. If someone insults him, he should say, 'I am fasting.'"*[79] This teaches Muslims to dispute only when necessary, and to do so in the way that is pleasing to Allah ﷻ.

A WARNING AGAINST TRANSGRESSING THE BOUNDS

Unfortunately, certain Muslim factions are ignorant of the etiquette that should be shown when a difference of opinion arises. This leads them to transgress, insult others, or accuse them of innovation or disbelief. The reality is that those they insult may have better etiquette with Allah ﷻ and more commitment to the Sunna of His Messenger ﷺ than they do! The accuser perhaps has a limited understanding based on what he had heard in a lecture or read in a book, but the religion is broader than his limited understanding. He would do well to examine and follow the statements of the first generations and those who followed them with excellence, which clarify the reality of this matter.

---

78 Narrated by al-Tirmidhī who categorized it as *Ḥasan Ṣaḥīḥ,* by Aḥmad in *al-Musnad*, Ibn Māja, and al-Ḥākim in *al-Mustadrak* on the authority of Abū Umāma.

Translator's note: Another understanding of the Hadith, as stated by Mullā 'Alī Qārī in his commentary on *Mishkāt al-Maṣābīḥ,* would translate as, *"People go astray after receiving guidance only when they take to disputing."* As Mullā 'Alī Qārī states, "Their misguidance and falling into disbelief was **due to disputing** (*jadal*), which was arguing with falsehood against their Prophet and requesting miracles from him out of stubbornness and rejection." [*Mirqāt al-Mafātīḥ Sharḥ Mishkāt al-Maṣābīḥ,* Hadith 180, emphasis added]

79 Narrated by al-Bukhārī in *Kitāb al-Ṣawm* (Hadith 1805), and by Muslim in *Kitāb al-Ṣiyām* (Hadith 1151).

The devil exploits a person's haste and fanaticism, making him believe that his anger is for Allah's sake ﷻ, when in reality, his anger is caused by his own misunderstandings and shortsightedness. He is so deluded that he even considers it permissible to violate another person's honor, and maybe even his life and wealth.

This is the same mistake made by the people who fought against the Companions of Allah's Messenger ﷺ, whom we have been commanded explicitly in the Quran to follow.[80] **"As for the foremost—the first of the Emigrants and the Helpers—and *those who follow them* with excellence."** [Quran 9:100]

What is even stranger is that these same people justified their actions by taking verses about the disbelievers in Mecca and applied them to the Companions! The Companions were persecuted because of their belief in Allah ﷻ, yet that group accused them of disbelief and misguidance, concluding that it was permissible to fight them, kill them, and take their wealth. We seek refuge in Allah ﷻ.

We must therefore be extremely wary of disputation that fans the flames of sedition and judges others based on subjective interpretations. Muslims must have a sound understanding of the different legal schools and valid perspectives within the religion. Rulings that are based on well-founded religious principles bring about unity, and interpretations that cause division only result from the ignorance of those who do not understand the religious methodology followed by scholars.

MAINTAINING ETIQUETTES OF DIFFERENCE

Valid differences of opinion can occur without there being sectarian conflicts and hatred between people's hearts. Differences of opinion occur when those who have the capacity to study the Quran and Hadith

80 Translator's note: this is in reference to the Khawārij, who fought against the Companions and accused them of disbelief.

come to different conclusions regarding some of the text's indications. This is part of Allah's wisdom in placing breadth within the Sacred Law, as people have varied needs and different things benefit different people. This allows for various perspectives on the authoritative texts that branch out into various understandings.

The noble Companions differed without any of them finding fault in the other or deeming the other's conclusion as false or contradicting the text. Each Companion recognized that the other Companion was qualified to understand the text, despite having a different perspective and understanding than his own. There are many examples of this in the lives of the Companions, the Followers (*Tābiʿīn*) who came after them, and the subsequent generations. They were all sincere and adhered to the etiquettes of the Sharia.

One of our obligations within the Kingdom of the Heart is to not allow differences of opinion on secondary issues to cause hatred. We must understand that it is precisely due to the breadth of the Sharia that the various rightly guided schools were established. Their foundations are the Quran, Sunna, and consensus of the Companions, the Followers, and those who came after them. When the foundations are sound, it becomes easy for people to accept other valid positions and not recklessly accuse others of misguidance. Firmly established religious principles unify people's hearts.

With tolerance and mutual understanding, Muslims are even able to work with the broader community to rectify society. If they are able to work with the people of other faiths, then it only makes sense that they should be able to work even more closely with other Muslims. There are many issues that all Muslims agree on, so they should collectively strive to address them. These include promoting virtue, preventing harm, fulfilling obligations, avoiding prohibitions, benefitting society, taking care of the needy, etc. Muslims cannot neglect these things nor allow differences of opinion on secondary issues to divide them or cause them to disparage each other.

We ask Allah ﷾ to enable the believers to have etiquette with Him, which then leads them to fulfill the rights of others, honor them, and think well of every Muslim. We then become beautified through good manners that make us speak well of one another and elevate us above conflict. May Allah ﷾ make us steadfast upon what He loves, include us among those He loves, and protect us from evil. May Allah's peace and blessings be upon the Chosen One, Muhammad, and upon his Family and Companions. All praise belongs to Allah, Lord of the Worlds.

CHAPTER 17

The Heart & Limbs Collectively Acquire the Greater Kingdom

All praise belongs to Allah, Lord of the Worlds. Praise belongs to Him in every state, condition, and moment. There is no god except Him ﷻ. He created us and to Him is the ultimate end. He sent His Servant, the bearer of glad tidings, the warner, and the luminous lamp—Muhammad ﷺ—with guidance. May Allah's peace and blessings be upon him, his Family, Companions, and all who follow his path until the Day of Judgment.

To proceed: As mentioned previously, what we do with our hands has a significant impact on the Kingdom of the Heart. Striking others, as we explained, results in retribution on the Day of Resurrection. Allah ﷻ holds people accountable for a slap and anything more severe. Even hitting an animal wrongfully is something one accounts for on the Day of Resurrection.

If a hornless sheep takes its due from a horned one, then what standard is a morally accountable person held to? The Prophet ﷺ said in an authentic Hadith, *"A woman was punished for her treatment of a cat. She kept it locked up until it died, so she entered the Fire for that. When she locked it up, she did not give it food or water, nor did she let it go out to eat stray rodents."*[81] Whenever someone hits a person or animal in a way that

81 Narrated by al-Bukhārī in *Kitāb al-Musāqā* (Hadith 2236), and Muslim in *Kitāb*

is not permitted by Allah ﷻ, he will be questioned, held accountable, and the rights of the one harmed will be taken from him.

With that being said, we are also told of the reward for striking in Allah's cause ﷻ. We mentioned previously that the Prophet ﷺ never struck a man, woman, or child, and that he only used force when fighting in Allah's cause.

When someone loves Allah ﷻ and offers his own soul for His cause sincerely and with a sound intention, then his actions with his hands become a means for attaining a higher degree and more elevated rank with Allah ﷻ. In doing so, he resists the inclinations and desires of the lower self, prefers his Lord's reward, and seeks to attain true servitude by fulfilling his covenant with Allah.

THE BATTLE OF BADR

In the face of hostile and oppressive forces that sought to stand against the truth during the Great Battle of Badr, the light of Prophetic virtue shone brightly. In this momentous battle, which took place on the 17th of Ramadan in the 2nd year after the Hijra, we see how the Companions used the entirety of their limbs in the noblest of ways.

The Decisive Day, when the two armies met in battle, is an occasion full of values and lessons for those with purified souls.[82] It teaches the Ummah how to be true and sincere with Allah ﷻ, act with excellence, and show humility, modesty, and forbearance in the face of arrogance and enmity—and it shows the ultimate outcomes of each of those things.

The People of Badr attained lofty degrees by way of their hands, which were supported by all their limbs, as well as by the ruler of the Kingdom, the heart. The Companions went out sincerely seeking Allah's

---

al-Salām and in *Kitāb al-Birr wa'l Ṣila* (Hadith 2242).

82 Translator's note: See Quran 8:41.

Countenance ﷺ. Prior to the battle, the Messenger of Allah ﷺ consulted them after the enemy's caravan had passed and their army was coming out to meet them. Abu Bakr ؓ spoke excellently, as did ʿUmar ؓ. Then Miqdād ؓ said, "O Messenger of Allah! By Allah, we will not say to you what the Tribes of Isrāʾīl said to Mūsā, 'Go, you and your Lord, and fight. We are staying right here.' Rather, we say, 'Go, you and your Lord, and fight—we will fight with you!' By Allah, we will fight in front of you, behind you, and to your right and left."

This made the Messenger of Allah ﷺ extremely happy and his face lit up, but to be sure with respect to the Anṣār, he asked the group once again, *"Give me your counsel."* Saʿd ibn Muʿādh ؓ, a man of sincerity, tremendous determination, and who preferred Allah and His Messenger over all else, understood what the Prophet ﷺ was asking. He said, "O Messenger of Allah, it is as if you are directing your question to us, the Anṣār."

He then delivered his momentous speech, which was filled with sublime meanings, "O Messenger of Allah! We believe in and affirm that the message you have brought is true. We have taken oaths and given you our pledge on that basis. Therefore, go wherever Allah has commanded you. There are people who stayed behind in Madina who have just as much love for you as we do. Had they known that you were to engage in battle, they would not have stayed behind. Perhaps you wanted something, yet Allah willed something else.

"Go wherever you want, for by Allah, if you were to take us until we reached Birk al-Ghimād in Abyssinia, we would go with you and not one man would stay behind. If you took us to the sea and plunged in, we would dive in with you. We have no fear of meeting the enemy. We are steadfast in war and unwavering in battle."

The Prophet's face ﷺ lit up like the moon, and he said, *"Continue onwards and take this good news that brings you joy: Allah has promised me victory over one of the two groups—either the caravan or the army. By Allah, it is as if I am now looking at the places where the enemy will fall.*"[83]

THE RESULT OF RECTIFYING THE HEART

Many amazing events occurred during this battle. The uprightness of their hearts—the Kingdom's ruler—translated to the uprightness of their limbs. Those who were present at the Battle of Badr were the best people on earth. At a later time, the Angel Jibrīl ﷺ asked the Prophet ﷺ, "What standing do the People of Badr have amongst you?" The Prophet ﷺ said, *"They are the best of the Muslims,"* or something to that effect. Jibrīl then said, "We hold the angels who attended Badr in the same esteem."[84] Allah ﷻ raised their rank because they attended the battle with His Prophet ﷺ.

The Battle of Badr was filled with wondrous miracles and signs because the Companions embodied true servitude (*'ubūdīyya*) to the Lord of the heavens and the earth ﷻ. One of the wonders that occurred was due to their abundant and emphatic supplication (*du'ā*), which is an action of the tongue that is connected to the heart. *Du'ā* is considered worship[85] because it directs the heart exclusively towards the One being supplicated to: Allah ﷻ. *Du'ā* is an expression of a person's complete need of his Lord ﷻ, making it a means to attain Allah's assistance and mercy.

Allah ﷻ says when mentioning this battle, **"When you cried out to your Lord for help, He answered, 'I will reinforce you with a thousand angels—followed by many others.'"** [Quran 8:9] When they cried out

83 Narrated by Ibn Isḥāq in his *Maghāzī*, supported by Hadiths in the two *Ṣaḥīḥ* collections and others.

84 Narrated by al-Bukhārī in *Kitāb al-Maghāzī* (Hadith 3771).

85 The Hadith, *"Supplication* (du'ā) *is worship"* is narrated by Aḥmad in his *Musnad*, by Ibn Abī Shayba, al-Bukhārī in his book *al-Adab*, and in the four books of Sunna: Abū Dawūd, al-Tirmidhī, al-Nasā'ī, and Ibn Māja. It is also narrated by Ibn Ḥibbān in his *Ṣaḥīḥ* and al-Ḥākim in *al-Mustadrak* on the authority of al-Nu'mān ibn Bashīr.

to Allah ﷻ in a state of broken-heartedness and humbleness before Him, Allah's assistance came.

One of the Prophet's miracles ﷺ that occurred before the battle was that he identified the places where the enemy would fall. Nevertheless, he spent the entire night emphatically and persistently calling upon Allah ﷻ, which shows us that one of the best uses of the tongue is to make *du'ā*. It is incumbent upon us that we persistently call upon Allah, ask Him abundantly, and humble ourselves before Him ﷻ.

THE IMPACT OF UPRIGHTNESS

When we understand that actions are influenced by the heart, we realize that our Kingdom is dependent upon the uprightness of its ruler. Each of us has a Kingdom that leads us either to the great and everlasting dominion or to everlasting and humiliating loss—and we seek refuge in Allah ﷻ from that. Purify the seat of leadership within you, which is your heart, from the filth that afflicts it and then spreads to all of the body's limbs.

Carefully study the states of those whose hearts became pure, such as 'Umayr ibn al-Ḥumām ؓ. When he heard the Messenger of Allah ﷺ say, *"Rise to a Garden that is as expansive as the heavens and earth!"* he said, "O Messenger of Allah, a Garden that is as expansive as the heavens and the earth?" He said, *"Yes."* 'Umayr said, "How excellent!" Then the Messenger of Allah ﷺ said, *"What made you say, 'How excellent'?"* He replied, "By Allah, O Messenger of Allah, I only said it out of hope that I may be one of its people." The Messenger of Allah replied, *"You are certainly of its people."* 'Umayr then took some dates out of his bag and began to eat them. Then he said, "If I live long enough to eat these dates, then that is too long!" He cast aside the dates and fought until he was killed.[86]

Your hopes might be attached to this fleeting world, so reflect on

86 Narrated by Muslim in *Kitāb al-Imāra* (Hadith 1901).

how this sincere person felt it too long to eat the dates in his hand! This is because of what he experienced spiritually and came to know. Look at what happened to his heart when he heard what the Prophet had said. He formed that resolve after hearing the Prophet's declaration ﷺ, and he became one of the fourteen who were martyred on the Day of Badr—may Allah be well pleased with them all.

Allah ﷾ said, **"Indeed, Allah made you victorious at Badr when you were outnumbered. So be mindful of Allah, so that you may be grateful."** [Quran 3:123]

O Allah, grant us gratitude and allow us to use our bodies in ways that bring us closer to You. Protect us from the evil of our own selves. O Allah, make excellent our end and return to You, by Your mercy, O Most Merciful! May Allah's peace and blessings be upon the Chosen One, Muhammad, his Family, and Companions. All praise belongs to Allah, Lord of the Worlds.

CHAPTER 18

Heavenly Ambitions & Objectives

All praise belongs to Allah,

> **He is Highly Exalted in rank, Lord of the Throne. He sends down the revelation by His command to whoever He wills of His servants to warn of the Day of Meeting—the Day all will appear ˹before Him˺. Nothing about them will be hidden from Allah. ˹He will ask,˺ 'Who does all authority belong to this Day? To Allah—the One, the Supreme! Today every soul will be rewarded for what it has done. Today, no injustice will be done. Surely Allah is swift in reckoning.'**
> [Quran 40:15–17]

We bear witness there is no god except Allah, One without partner. And we bear witness that our master Muhammad ﷺ is His Servant and Messenger. He excellently conveyed the Message and fulfilled the trust. He invited to Allah with clear proofs and those with illuminated inner sights responded to him. May Allah's peace and blessings be upon him, and upon his Family, Companions, and all those who follow his guidance until the Day of Judgment.

To proceed: A person's purpose, will, and aspiration, which are contained within his heart, have an immense impact on his limbs. The limbs obey the heart to actualize these objectives. When one's aspirations become rarified and elevated, they cause his soul to elevate and ascend.

THE IMPACT OF HIGH ASPIRATIONS

When we discussed the great Battle of Badr in the previous chapter, we saw how elevated the aspirations of the Companions were. This teaches us how to attain distinction by way of sublime aspirations, for both us and our families. It also helps us identify the aspirations and ideals that have been lost within the Ummah. Those who come to know the greatest objective are never content with settling for anything less. This is what elevated the ranks of the Companions ﷺ.

We find great meanings expressed by al-Miqdād, Saʿd ibn Muʿādh, and ʿUmayr ibn al-Ḥumām ﷺ. These understandings reached even the hearts of the young Companions. Some of those present at Badr were at the early stage of their youth, around fifteen years old.

Muʿādh and Muʿawwidh the sons of ʿAfrāʾ ﷺ were two youths who were young in age, yet great in the loftiness of their aspirations. They were standing by ʿAbd al-Raḥmān ibn ʿAwf ﷺ in battle, who said, "When the army formed ranks for battle, I saw a young boy to my right and another young boy to my left, which made me feel unsafe. Then the person to my right whispered, 'Uncle, do you know which of them is Abū Jahl?' I said, 'Yes.' He said, 'I ask that you point him out to me if we see him during battle.' I said, 'My nephew, what do you want with him?' He replied, 'I was told that he used to harm Allah's Messenger. I swear by the One who reigns over my soul that if I see him, I will not stop attacking him until one of us is dead.' I was amazed by his faith and strong resolve. Then the other young boy spoke to me, asked me the same question, and gave me the same answer. I would not have preferred two large and powerful men in their stead."

Look at the loftiness of their aim! They had no worldly advantage to gain from Abū Jahl. They were driven only by love for Allah and His Messenger ﷺ and servitude to Him ﷻ. Abū Jahl was a leader of the disbelievers who fought against the Messenger, sought to drive him out, and caused extensive harm and evil. They hoped to save people from those who exerted their utmost to transgress against truth and guidance, thereby giving them a chance to be guided to truth, goodness, and light.

During the battle, ʿAbd al-Raḥmān ibn ʿAwf رضي الله عنه saw Abū Jahl then said to the two of them, "There he is." ʿAbd al-Raḥmān ibn ʿAwf said, describing them, "They were like two falcons swooping upon their prey." They struck him until he fell, after which they went to the Messenger of Allah ﷺ to give him the good news of the demise of this tyrant. Look at the aspirations of these two young men, who were in the prime of their youth. They had this kind of resolve because the lights of Prophethood and revelation permeated and impacted their souls. As a community of believers who testify in the truthfulness of the Messenger of Allah ﷺ, we should be impacted in the same way. What are the aspirations of our fifteen, sixteen, and seventeen-year-old men and women?

Another Companion who was present at the battle was a young man who was seventeen or eighteen years old, the martyr of exalted rank, Ḥāritha ibn Surāqa رضي الله عنه. He was his mother's only child. This righteous young man exemplifies the sublime aspirations found within the hearts of the people of purity, goodness, and nobility. This is evident from the fact that he asked the Messenger of Allah to make *duʿā* that he be a martyr. The Prophet ﷺ then said, *"O Allah, grant Ḥāritha martyrdom in Your cause."*

Ḥāritha was present at the Battle of Badr and was one of the fourteen who were martyred. When the Messenger of Allah ﷺ returned to Madina, Ḥāritha's mother came to him and asked, "O Messenger of Allah, you know how precious Ḥāritha is to me, and he is my only child. Where is my son, Ḥāritha?" He replied, *"Consider him with Allah. He was killed in the cause of Allah."* She requested again, "Tell me where my son is." The Prophet responded, *"I am telling you that he was killed in the cause of Allah, so consider him with Allah."* Finally, she said, "I am asking you where my son is: if he is in the Garden, then I will be patient; if it is otherwise, then what shall I do?" The Prophet ﷺ replied, *"Mercy on you, O Mother of Ḥāritha! Paradise does not have just one Garden, but many Gardens—and your son has attained the Highest Garden of Firdaws."*[87]

This young man's ultimate goal was nearness to Allah ﷾, His good pleasure, and everlasting bliss—all of which he attained. He was one of the sincere and true People of Badr, who were the best of the Companions. May Allah ﷾ be well pleased with them.

The Battle of Badr was full of wonders, showing that having lofty aims is a virtue that must be firmly rooted in the hearts of Muslims. This is how we overcome the problems that are destabilizing the Ummah. The problems that the Ummah is facing occur when greed, worldly desire, and forgetting the return to Allah ﷾ take over. When people's main concern is to acquire worldly things, they go astray and transgress, even if they might believe that their actions are rightly guided.

BEING TRUE WITH ALLAH ﷾

Being true with Allah ﷾ removes one's hope in the fleeting and superficial things of this life. He says ﷾, **"That Home in the Hereafter We reserve for those who seek neither superiority on the earth nor corruption. The ultimate outcome belongs to the righteous."** [Quran 28:83] By desiring neither superiority nor corruption on the earth, those who are true with Allah ﷾ are given superiority in both the heavens and the earth, in this life and in the next. They are the righteous and successful, and Allah elevates their rank due to their trueness and sincerity with Him ﷾.

87 Narrated by al-Bukhārī in *Kitāb al-Jihād* (Hadith 2654).

Sa'd ibn Mu'ādh ﵁ said to the Messenger of Allah ﷺ when they faced the army at Badr, "O Messenger of Allah, shall we build a shelter for you and place your camel close to you while we meet the enemy? If Allah gives us victory over them and honors us, then this is the outcome we would love. If the other outcome occurs, then you can mount your steed and return to our people who have remained behind. By Allah, there are people who stayed behind ⌜in Madina⌝ who love you just as intensely as we do. Had they known that you were going to engage in battle, they would not have stayed behind, and they would have supported and assisted you." The Messenger of Allah ﷺ then praised him and made *du'ā* for him. A shelter was then constructed for him, and the Messenger of Allah ﷺ stayed there with Abū Bakr al-Ṣiddīq ﵁ as his guard.

The Messenger of Allah ﷺ spent the night before the battle in intense supplication and prostration. The next morning, after Ḥamza ibn 'Abd al-Muṭṭalib ﵁ dueled against 'Utba ibn Rabī'a, Imam 'Alī ibn Abū Ṭālib ﵁ against Shayba ibn Rabī'a, and 'Ubayda ibn al-Ḥārith ﵁ against al-Walīd, Allah ﷻ revealed, **"These are two opposing groups who disputed about their Lord."** [Quran 22:19]

In the authentic Hadith, the Prophet ﷺ said, *"The first thing to be judged between people on the Day of Resurrection is related to the shedding of blood."*[88] Regarding this, Imam 'Alī ibn Abū Ṭālib ﵁ said, "I will be the first to kneel before Allah regarding the dispute."[89] He was referring to the verse, **"These are two opposing groups who disputed about their Lord,"** which was revealed about his group dueling against the disbelievers prior to Badr. Both groups will be asked about their motives for fighting in that battle.

This shows us that Allah ﷻ will question every fighter about his motivations for setting out in Jihad. This is further illustrated in the

88 Narrated by al-Bukhārī in *Kitāb al-Dīyāt* (Hadith 6471), and by Muslim in *Kitāb al-Qisāma wa'l Muḥāribīn wa'l Qiṣāṣ wa'l Dīyāt* (Hadith 1678).

89 Narrated by Muslim in *Kitāb al-Tafsīr* (Hadith 3033).

Hadiths, *"Allah knows best the intention of someone who was killed in the ranks."*[90] And, *"If someone sets out to battle intending* ˹to *acquire*˺ *a rope to hobble a camel, then he receives only what he intended."*[91] Out of the entire reward for the battle, he only receives a piece of rope.[92]

Therefore, our objectives must be exalted. The Prophet ﷺ was asked, "O Messenger of Allah, a man fights for the spoils of war, another out of tribalism, and yet another fights to show his valor. Which of them is striving in the way of Allah? He said ﷺ, *"Whoever fights so that Allah's Word is supreme, he is in the way of Allah."*[93] The one whose intention was solely seeking Allah's Noble Countenance, who rose above ulterior motives, desires, and seeking superiority in the earth—he is in the way of Allah ﷻ.

We see how, on the Day of Badr, Allah gave victory to the smaller army that had much less military power,

> **Indeed, Allah made you victorious at Badr when you were ˹vastly˺ outnumbered. Be mindful of Allah, so that you may be grateful. ˹Remember, O Prophet,˺ when you said to the believers, 'Is it not enough that your Lord will send down a reinforcement of three thousand angels to your aid?' Most certainly, if you are firm and mindful ˹of Allah˺ and the enemy launches a sudden attack on you, Allah will reinforce you with five thousand designated angels. Allah ordained this only as good news for you and reassurance for your hearts. And victory comes only from Allah—the Almighty, All-Wise.**
> [Quran 3:123–126]

90 Narrated by Aḥmad on the authority of Ibn Mas'ūd.

91 Narrated by Ahmad in his *Musnad*, al-Nasā'ī, and al-Ḥākim in *al-Mustadrak* on the authority of 'Ubāda ibn al-Ṣāmit.

92 Translator's note: A camel hobble (*'iqāl*), is a rope that is used to tie a camel's legs to keep it stationary.

93 Narrated by al-Bukhārī in *Kitāb al-Tawḥīd* (Hadith 7020), and by Muslim in *Kitāb al-Imāra* (Hadith 1904).

And Allah ﷻ said, **"If Allah helps you, none can defeat you. But if He forsakes you, then who else can help you?"** [Quran 3:160]

After the battle ended and the polytheists fled, the Prophet ﷺ preserved the enemy's dignity. Seventy were killed and seventy more were taken prisoner. The Prophet ﷺ commanded that their dead be buried and not left to vultures or predatory beasts. We must appreciate the nobility of his consideration to bury the corpses of hostile disbelievers who fought against him. These exemplify the character traits and etiquettes of Islam.

He ﷺ then stood over their graves and said, *"O Abū Jahl ibn Hishām, O Umayya ibn Khalaf, O ʿUtba ibn Rabīʿa, O Shayba ibn Rabīʿa—did you find your Lord's promise to be true? For I have certainly found what my Lord has promised me to be true."* ʿUmar ibn al-Khaṭṭāb ؓ asked the Prophet, "Why are you addressing lifeless bodies?" He replied, *"By the One in whose hand is Muhammad's soul, they hear what I am saying just as well as you do."*[94]

The Muslims brought back the prisoners to Madina and the Messenger of Allah ﷺ requested that they be treated well. The Companions ؓ then gave them preference over themselves by offering their prisoners the best food. This was the state of the noble Companions and their understanding of fulfilling others' rights and treating prisoners humanely.

O Allah, allow us to follow their path, unite us with them in the Abode of Honor while You are well-pleased with us, and do not separate us from them on the Day of Resurrection—O Most Merciful! May Allah's peace and blessings be upon our master Muhammad, his Family, Companions, and all those who follow his path. All praise belongs to Allah, Lord of the Worlds.

94 Narrated by al-Bukhārī in *Kitāb al-Maghāzī* (Hadith 3757), and by Muslim in *Kitāb al-Janna wa Ṣifat Naʿīmihā wa Ahlihā* (Hadith 2875).

CHAPTER 19

Commemorating Blessed Times of the Year

All praise belongs to Allah, the Noblest Sovereign. May Allah's peace and blessings be upon His Servant, the Chosen One, Muhammad, possessor of the utmost honor, and upon his Family, Companions, and those who faithfully follow his path.

To proceed: As Muslims, we have many blessed days and months in our calendar. Commemorating them impacts the Kingdom of the Heart. During these blessed times, we should experience a set of emotional responses that strengthen our commitment to Allah ﷻ and help purify us. This, in turn, impacts our actions.

We should welcome these virtuous times with the appropriate sentiments that correspond to each of them. There are entire Muslim families who are completely oblivious to the blessings that Allah ﷻ has placed in these times. This is a manifestation of immense heedlessness. In the Book of Allah, we are told about the significance of the lunar months, **"They ask you ˹O Prophet˺ about the phases of the moon. Say, 'They are a means for people to determine time and pilgrimage.'"** [Quran 2:189]

DISTINCTIONS OF THE MONTHS

Allah ﷻ made four of the months sacred,[95] and He made the month of Ramadan preeminent over all other months. He taught us some aspects of Ramadan's significance when He ﷻ said, **"Ramadan is the month in which the Quran was revealed as a guide for humanity with clear proofs of guidance and the distinguishing between right and wrong."** [Quran 2:185] He also decreed that the Battle of Badr and Conquest of Mecca would occur in Ramadan. Allah ﷻ placed the obligation of fasting and the Sunna of night worship in Ramadan. Allah made Ramadan the time when people are emancipated from the Fire. In each of Ramadan's nights and days, and especially at the times of sunset and sunrise. Six-hundred thousand people are emancipated from the Fire every night of Ramadan. At the end of the month, Allah frees an amount equal to the sum total of the people freed from the beginning of the month to its end.[96]

Throughout the noble month of Ramadan, we find new opportunities for reward and self-rectification. The last ten nights of Ramadan were given a distinction over the other nights. Additionally, the Night of Great Worth (*Laylat al-Qadr*) most often occurs within the last ten nights of Ramadan. When we recognize all of the blessings in Ramadan, it evokes a sentiment that encourages us to be well-prepared for it. During the last ten nights of Ramadan, our Prophet ﷺ tightened his waistcloth, gave life to its nights with worship, and awakened his family to pray at night.[97]

---

95 Translator's note: The four sacred months are Rajab, Dhu'l Qiʿda, Dhu'l Ḥijja, and Muḥarram.

96 As narrated by al-Bayhaqī in *Shuʿab al-Imān,* and by al-Aṣbahānī in *al-Targhīb* on the authority of al-Ḥasan.

97 As narrated by al-Bukhārī in *Kitāb Ṣalāt al-Tarāwīḥ* (Hadith 1920), and by Muslim *Kitāb al-Iʿtikāf* (Hadith 1174).

Translator's note: "tightened his waistcloth" could be an expression of his seriousness and determination during the last ten nights or could indicate that he would refrain from approaching his wives during that time.

He emphasized the exceptional nature of those nights by intensifying his worship and devotion.

When the month ends, taking all of its spiritual breezes and gifts with it, we then welcome Eid al-Fiṭr with expressing our gratitude to Allah ﷻ. **"Complete the prescribed period and proclaim the greatness of Allah for guiding you, so that you may be thankful."** [Quran 2:185] Immediately after Ramadan, we welcome the following month, which provides us with the opportunity to fast the six days of Shawwāl. As we leave one time of worship, we are met with another time of worship, which prevents us from interrupting our devotion to Allah ﷻ. In *Ṣaḥīḥ Muslim* the Prophet ﷺ said, *"Whoever fasts Ramadan and follows it with six days of Shawwāl, it is like fasting the entire year."*[98]

After the month of Shawwāl, we enter Dhu'l Qiʿda, which is one of the sacred months. Dhu'l Ḥijja follows, and in addition to being a sacred month, is also the month when the Hajj takes place. The year then comes to an end, and we welcome a new Hijri year in which we commemorate our Prophet Muhammad's migration ﷺ.

In Rabīʿ al-Awwal, we commemorate our Messenger's birth ﷺ and emergence into the world. Then the month of Rajab comes, a singular sacred month that is neither preceded nor followed by another sacred month. In Rajab, we commemorate our beloved Prophet's Night Journey and Heavenly Ascent (*al-Isrāʾ wa'l Miʿrāj*). The month of Shaʿbān then follows, which contains the 15th night (*Laylat al-Niṣf*). Many Hadiths have been narrated about the significance of the blessed 15th night of Shaʿbān. After that, the month of Ramadan comes again.

Throughout the year we have opportunities to renew these sentiments and benefit accordingly from these blessed times. When the Prophet ﷺ found the Jews in Madina fasting on the Day of ʿĀshūrāʾ, he asked them why they were doing so. They said, "This is the day when Allah gave

98 Narrated by Muslim in *Kitāb al-Ṣiyām* (Hadith 1164).

Mūsā victory over the Pharaoh. We fast it out of respect for him." The Prophet ﷺ said, *"We have a stronger connection to Mūsā than you."* He then fasted that day and told the people to fast as well.[99]

The Prophet's wisdom in commemorating these great events is that they inspire us to turn to Allah ﷻ and renew our commitment to Him. If Ramadan, the sacred months, the Hajj season, and the Day of 'Ashūrā' all come and go, and yet a believer is apathetic about purifying himself and taking himself to account, this is a sign that his heart is dead. Heedlessness has seized the hearts and minds of many Muslims, weakening their attachment to these blessed days and the events that occurred during them.

THE PROPHET'S CONCERN FOR TIME

Our Prophet Muhammad ﷺ set the most remarkable example of how to experience these blessed times and give them their due. He exemplified what it means to renew our covenant with and orientation to Allah ﷻ. This is all within our reach if we are sincere and not swayed by lowly motives and base desires. When we rise above these desires, our hearts may then discover the unique merits and spiritual gifts that Allah ﷻ has placed within these blessed days and nights throughout the year.

We see this with the Prophet's sentiments ﷺ on a weekly basis when he fasted on Mondays and Thursdays, the days that actions are presented to Allah. He said ﷺ, *"I love for my actions to be presented while I am fasting."*[100]

In addition, the Prophet ﷺ would fast frequently in the month of Sha'bān, emphasizing that actions are presented to Allah ﷻ during this month and that it is a blessed month that many neglect. In another

99 Narrated by Abū Dawūd in *Kitāb al-Ṣiyām* (Hadith 2444).

100 The full Hadith states: *"Actions and presented on Mondays and Thursdays, so I would love for my actions to be presented while I am fasting."* [Narrated by al-Tirmidhī and al-Nasā'ī]

Hadith, the Prophet ﷺ said, *"The best fast after Ramadan is during Allah's sacred month (Muḥarram)."*[101]

He also taught us to fast the White Days that coincide with the full moon.[102] This monthly act of worship teaches us to be attuned to the cosmos and connects us to our Creator ﷻ.

When the disciples of Jesus ﷺ requested that he ask Allah ﷻ to send down a table spread from heaven, he said, **"'O Allah, our Lord! Send us a table spread from heaven, which will be a celebration for us—the first and last of us.'"** [Quran 5:114] What is meant by a 'celebration' for the first and last of them? The table spread came down for the people who were present that day and they ate from it once, and that was all. But Jesus ﷺ said, **"Which will be a celebration for us—the first and the last of us."** This means that the memory of this extraordinary event will remain for later generations because of its connection to the One Who brought the table spread down from heaven. **"Allah answered, 'I am sending it down to you. But whoever among you disbelieves afterwards will be subjected to a torment I have never inflicted on anyone of My creation.'"** [Quran 5:115] In other words, Allah is saying: such a threat of punishment is promised because the proof is undeniable, and I have shown you a miracle and favored you.

In Jesus's statement ﷺ, **"Which will be a celebration for us—the first and the last of us,"** there is a clear indication of the sentiments evoked by recurring commemorations. Later generations continue to remember what happened to the first generations, and this is illustrated in the Sunna when the Prophet ﷺ commemorated the Day of 'Ashūrā' and said, *"We have a stronger connection to Mūsā than you."*

101 Narrated by Muslim in *Kitāb al-Ṣiyām* (Hadith 1163).

102 Translators note: these are the 13th, 14th, and 15th of each lunar month.

EXPERIENCING COMMEMORATIONS

The commemorations recognized by the Master of Messengers ﷺ are more deserving of consideration and worthier of evoking sentiments within our hearts. These sentiments flowed through the hearts of the noble Companions ﷺ.

The Prophet's uncle, Al-ʿAbbās ibn ʿAbd al-Muṭṭalib ﷺ, spoke in verse, praising the Prophet Muhammad ﷺ and expressing his feelings about the Prophet's noble birth. He said, "I want to praise you." The Prophet ﷺ answered him, *"Go ahead, may Allah bless your speech."* So al-ʿAbbās said,

> When you were born, the earth and horizons
> were illuminated with your light!
> We remain bathed in that radiance
> as it lights the path for us[103]

Al-ʿAbbās ﷺ made the connection between the light of guidance and the light that emanated at his birth ﷺ.

For the believers, the heart finds its foundation in the sentiments connected to these commemorations. These commemorations produce insights, spiritual experiences, and profound understandings within the heart. They illuminate one's heart and conscience. One accesses the fruits of these blessed occasions by having proper manners with the Sacred Law, uprightness, and by rectifying one's speech, actions, and states.

Also, these commemorations inspire us to fulfill our duties, which are the basis for our felicity. For example, these commemorations inspire our hands to engage in donating and giving. They motivate our tongues to engage in beautiful *dhikr*: praising, remembering, and thanking Allah ﷻ, and sending blessings upon the Messenger of Allah ﷺ. These commemorations inspire us to be cheerful, use kind words, and look at others with compassion and mercy. Such actions, among others, result

103 Narrated by al-Ḥākim in *al-Mustadrak,* and al-Ṭabarānī in *al-Kabīr*.

from these commemorations and from a profound understanding of their sublime meanings.

These sentiments provide the foundation for a meaningful connection to divine guidance. All people, not just those who are religious, use emotions to inspire people. They establish celebrations at certain times to commemorate events that they regard as significant. People require something to motivate them and reinforce their values, which is achieved through commemorations at specific times. This is the natural disposition that Allah ﷻ instilled within people, which is why evoking emotions that strengthen faith is a core part of our faith, as seen in the stories of the Prophets ﷺ. Allah ﷻ says, **"In their stories, there truly is a lesson for people of understanding."** [Quran 12:111] **"And We relate to you ˹O Prophet˺ the stories of the Messengers to strengthen your heart."** [Quran 11:120]

We ask Allah ﷻ to revive the proper associations with blessed times, seasons, and commemorations, so that we become connected to the Creator ﷻ in a way that strengthens our faith and certainty. Success is by Allah alone.

May Allah's peace and blessings be upon our master Muhammad and upon his Family and Companions. All praise belongs to Allah, Lord of the Worlds.

CHAPTER 20

What We Listen to Impacts Our Hearts

All praise belongs to Allah, Who gives generously and His favors are immense. May Allah's peace and blessings be upon His servant, the guide, our master Muhammad, and upon his Family and Companions who are the greatest of all families and companions.

To proceed: Our hearing plays an important role in the Kingdom of the Heart. Through hearing, we can expand our ability to think deeply, purify our intellects and lower selves, and gain a deeper understanding of spiritual realities. This distinctive quality is unique to hearing, which is connected to both the heart and intellect.

THE STATE OF THE UMMAH IN REFLECTING ON THE QURAN

Many people fall short in contemplating the Quran. Some are overly focused on perfecting their pronunciation that they become heedless of the meaning, resulting in a lack of humility, contemplation, and attentiveness of the heart. Others do not even have proper pronunciation, prattling quickly in their recitation, again without reflection or contemplation. Some are neglectful of reciting the Quran altogether, never opening the Mighty Book nor contemplating its meanings. Allah ﷻ

says regarding such people, **"The Messenger has cried, 'O my Lord! My people have indeed neglected this Quran.'"** [Quran 25:30] Additionally, there are those who limit themselves to a surface-level understanding of the Quran, holding back from diving into its vast ocean.

Imam 'Abd-Allāh al-Ḥaddād (may Allah have mercy on him) said,

> Be consistent in reciting the Quran, for doing so
> Brings tranquility and healing to the heart,
> Truly, it is the never-ending ocean, and other books
> Are merely rivers whose source is that ocean,
> Reflect upon it and recite it in a measured way with submissiveness
> For you will then receive a treasure of spiritual realities,
> Be fearful when hearing the threat of punishment
> And hopeful and joyful when hearing the promise of reward!

Failing to listen attentively to the Quran has caused many Muslims to suffer from a loss of certitude. The Messenger of Allah's words ﷺ, and even those of the wise, contain meanings that are continuously expanding. As we continue to ponder those statements, their meanings become inscribed within our hearts. If this is the case with the words of His servants, then what impact should Allah's Words ﷻ have on our hearts?

Not listening attentively to the Quran also weakens the Kingdom of the Heart. When we previously mentioned listening, we referenced the verse, **"So 'O Prophet', give good news to My servants—those who listen to what is said and follow the best of it."** [Quran 39:17–18] Allah ﷻ also says, **"There are truly signs in this for people who listen."** [Quran 10:67] And, **"And We seal their hearts so that they cannot hear."** [Quran 7:100] This shows that Allah made the state of the heart the basis for the ability to hear. Outward hearing is of no benefit if it fails to guide us towards discovering the truth.

We must contemplate the Quran regularly, understand its meanings with precision, and consistently revisit and examine it so that the treasures of its wisdom lead us to success. Allah ﷻ says, **"We have certainly made it easy to learn lessons from the Quran—so will anyone take heed?"** [Quran 54:17] He also says ﷻ, **"Will they not contemplate the Quran? Or are there locks upon their hearts?"** [Quran 47:24] Those who refuse to contemplate the Quran have locks upon their hearts, making them oblivious to admonitions and possibly even to their own selves.

Admonitions do not benefit passion's prisoner
Whose heart is locked and has deviated from the way,
He is arrogant, disregarding clear truth when it comes to him
Out of his excessive ignorance and aloofness,
Allah's Book is enough admonition for an intelligent person,
As mentioned in the Hadith of the greatest Master

THE RESULTS OF ATTENTIVELY LISTENING

Listening with contemplation is one of the essential etiquettes that we must have with Allah ﷻ, the One who blessed us with the faculty of hearing. For a person of concern, determination, and comprehension, listening attentively expands his understanding even in ordinary conversations with others. The Prophet ﷺ said, *"Wisdom is the lost property of the believer; wherever he finds it, he is most worthy of it."*[104] This is why a believer's ears are receptive to benefit even from the words of someone with limited knowledge. Many of this Kingdom's treasures are lost when one fails to listen in this way.

The Prophet ﷺ listened attentively to what was being said, and when he spoke, the listener could count his words.[105] He would sometimes repeat a sentence three times to ensure that those listening to him could

104 Narrated by al-Tirmidhī in *Abwāb al-ʿIlm* (Hadith 2828, and Ibn Māja in *Kitāb al-Zuhd* (Hadith 4169).

105 Narrated by al-Bukhārī on the authority of al-Sayyida ʿĀisha ؓ that when the Prophet ﷺ spoke, his words could be numbered, if someone counted them.

understand and retain what he said.[106] His gatherings were characterized by forbearance, modesty, and trustworthiness. Elders were treated with respect, youngsters with mercy, and Allah's boundaries would not be transgressed. In his gatherings, the Companions sat with such stillness that birds could have perched upon their heads. When he was silent, they spoke respectfully, never arguing in his presence. Whenever a Companion would speak, the rest would listen until he was finished.[107]

When the Messenger of Allah ﷺ requested that Ibn Mas'ūd ؓ recite some of the Quran to him, he responded, "How can I recite to you, when it was revealed to you?" The Prophet ﷺ replied, *"I love to hear it from others."*[108] The Prophet ﷺ enjoyed Ibn Mas'ūd's recitation. He ﷺ also said to Abū Mūsā al-Ash'arī ؓ, *"If only you had seen me when I was listening to your recitation last night. You have been given a beautiful voice like that of Dawūd!"*[109] Abū Mūsā ؓ said, "O Messenger of Allah, had I known you were there, I would have embellished it for you in the most elegant way!"[110] Meaning, "I would have gone to the fullest extent to adorn it so that I might attain your good pleasure, which contains my Lord's good pleasure."

There is great benefit when people listen attentively. On the other hand, when people do not listen to reminders, they forego numerous benefits and treasures, which are unattainable otherwise. The Words of the Creator ﷻ, the Lord of the heavens and earth, are most deserving of being listened to attentively and contemplated. Listening excellently to

---

106 Narrated by al-Tirmidhī in his *Sunan* on the authority of Anas ibn Mālik, who said, "The Messenger of Allah ﷺ would repeat a word three times so that he would be understood."

107 From a long hadith narrated by al-Ṭabarānī on the authority of Hind ibn Abī Hāla in which he described a collection of the Messenger of Allah's states ﷺ.

108 Narrated by al-Bukhārī in *Kitāb Faḍā'il al-Qur'ān* (Hadith 4762) and Muslim in *Kitāb Ṣalāt al-Musāfirīn* (Hadith 247).

109 Narrated by al-Bukhārī in *Kitāb Faḍā'il al-Qur'ān* (Hadith 4761) and Muslim in *Kitāb Ṣalāt al-Musāfirīn* (Hadith 793)—and the narration here is from Muslim.

110 This addition is narrated by al-Ḥākim in *al-Mustadrak,* al-Ṭabārānī in *al-Kabīr,* and Abū Ya'lā.

the Quran is a means for receiving mercy, as Allah ﷻ said, **"When the Quran is recited, listen to it attentively and be silent, so that you may be shown mercy."** [Quran 7:204] Therefore, we must encourage people to listen attentively, which has been absent from the lives of many Muslims.

PROTECTING ONE'S HEARING FROM FOUL LANGUAGE

We must protect ourselves from hearing foul language because it harms our hearts. This involves actively turning away from anything inappropriate. Furthermore, part of listening with excellence involves that we do not allow objectionable or useless remarks to settle in our hearts whatsoever. Even if we inadvertently hear something objectionable, after a few moments it should be as if we never heard it at all.

This is the way of those who know how to properly use the blessing of hearing. Despite listening to various kinds of speech, their state is as Allah ﷻ describes, **"When they hear frivolous talk, they turn away from it, saying, 'We are accountable for our deeds and you for yours. Peace be with you! We want nothing to do with those who act ignorantly.'"** [Quran 28:55] It is as if they never heard it to begin with, so it has no impact on their hearts. Even when encountering divergent opinions in a book or statements that deviate from the correct path, such people do not allow it to settle in their hearts, and as a result, it is as if they never read it. This is one of the reasons why we should learn from teachers and not rely on books alone.

> Books provide reminders for one with knowledge—
> But soundness and absurdity are both mixed within them

It is commonly said, "If someone's shaykh is a book, then he gets more wrong than he does right." The current state has harmed a lot of people. Matters have worsened to the point that various types of media are now people's teachers! We must reestablish the principle of acquiring knowledge from scholars who have deep understanding and who have received knowledge through authentic chains of transmission (*sanad*). This direct connection to scholars is irreplaceable. Many of these tools (books, audio lessons, etc.) are good for attaining benefit, understanding, and knowledge—however, we cannot depend on them exclusively. Rather, we need a connection to scholars so that we can ask them questions and discuss with them.

Allah ﷻ said, **"Ask those who have knowledge if you do not know."** [Quran 16:43] This is why the wise say, "To memorize two lines is better than reading two entire books, and two people studying together is even better than both."

Whoever takes knowledge directly from a Shaykh
  Is in a sanctuary, safe from deviation and distortion,
But whoever takes knowledge from books
  The learned consider his knowledge nonexistent

Another poet, bringing attention to this reality, said,

Knowledge is not in books and notes
  Rather, knowledge is in the hearts of men,
Whoever seeks knowledge on his own—
  Without a Shaykh—is sure to go astray

Ibn al-Mubārak famously said, "The *sanad* (chain of transmission) is part of the religion. Were it not for the *sanad*, anyone could say whatever they wanted to." Ibn Sīrīn also said, "Knowledge is religion, so examine well who you take your religion from." Imam Muslim regarded these statements as so crucial that he quoted them in his introduction to his *Ṣaḥīḥ* collection.

We ask Allah ﷻ for steadfastness, success, and uprightness. May Allah's peace and blessings be upon our master Muhammad, and upon his Family and Companions. All praise belongs to Allah, Lord of the Worlds.

CHAPTER 21

Speech Impacts One's Ultimate End

All praise belongs to Allah, the Sovereign, the Most Generous, the Most Giving. He sent His servant to us the Chosen One and best of creation, with guidance, truth, and direction. May Allah's peace, mercy, and blessings be upon him, his Family, Companions, and whoever follows his path until the Day of Calling Out.[111]

To proceed: Among the blessings bestowed upon is in this world—in fact the very purpose for which the heavens and the earth were created—is true knowledge. Allah ﷻ has said, **"Allah is the One Who created seven heavens, and likewise for the earth. The ⌜divine⌝ command descends between them *so you may know* that Allah is Most Capable of everything and that Allah certainly encompasses all things in ⌜His⌝ knowledge."** [Quran 65:12]

WORDS LEAD TO REWARD OR PUNISHMENT

Choosing one's words wisely has a far-reaching impact on the Kingdom of the Heart. Speech holds such significance that it can lead to either pun-

111 Translator's note: This is one of the names of the Day of Judgment. See Quran 40:32.

ishment or reward. Allah ﷾ has promised immense rewards for those who utter certain statements. He ﷾ says, **"So Allah will reward them for what they said with Gardens under which rivers flow, to stay there forever. And that is the reward of those who do good."** [Quran 5:85]

"So Allah will reward them *for what they said*," meaning that people will be given the greatest reward and entry into Paradise based on what they said. This is because words have a connection to the heart, to the realities of faith, and to a person's inner state. When we choose a good word and then vocalize it, this reflects the state of our hearts and true orientation. One's ultimate end and final return to Allah ﷾ depend on this.

After people take their places in Paradise or the Fire, a dialogue takes place between the people of the Fire and Allah ﷾: **"They will cry out, 'Our Lord! Our ill-fate took hold of us, so we became a misguided people. Our Lord! Take us out of this ˹Fire˺. Then if we ever go back to our old ways, we will truly be wrongdoers.'"** [Quran 23:106–107]

Allah states that among the reasons they entered the Fire was their ridiculing a praiseworthy supplication the believers would make,

> **Allah will say, "Be despised in there! Do not ˹ever˺ plead with Me ˹again˺! Indeed, there was a group of My servants who used to say, 'Our Lord! We have believed, so forgive us and have mercy on us, for You are the best of those who show mercy.'" But you were ˹so busy˺ mocking them that it made you forget My remembrance, and you used to laugh at them.** [Quran 23:108–110]

The people of Paradise are granted a great reward for the same words that the people of the Fire would mock. The believers would turn to Allah ﷾ abundantly through this supplication, **"Our Lord! We have believed, so forgive us and have mercy on us, for You are the best of those who show mercy."** This supplication was a confirmation of their faith and their way of seeking Allah's benevolence ﷾ so that He may forgive them and have mercy on them.

This is characteristic of most of the supplications that the righteous have regularly made throughout the centuries. Their turning to Allah ﷻ and statements are comprised of seeking mercy, forgiveness, and strengthening their faith. We see this in the following Quranic supplication, **"Our Lord! We have believed, so forgive us and have mercy on us, for You are the best of those who show mercy."** [Quran 23:109]

Allah ﷻ says, **"But you were ˹so busy˺ mocking them that it made you forget My remembrance, and you used to laugh at them."** [Quran 23:110] In other words, Allah is saying to the disbelievers: You were not moved by their supplication to remember your final return, nor did you reflect on your state and how you responded to Our revelation and guidance. Rather than evoking noble sentiments within you, you mocked their words out of deference to the whims of your lower selves. Their supplication was not in line with the transgression, misguidance, and impulses of the lower self that you gratified yourselves with. Your mocking them was only a result of the evil that had already settled in your hearts.

OUR RESPONSE TO WHAT WE HEAR REFLECTS OUR STATE

Certain statements capture our attention, and we find agreeable. While other statements are repulsive and contemptible. People's reaction to each reflects the states of the people of Paradise, the believers, and the people of the Fire, the disbelievers.

The believer who has reverence for Allah is naturally drawn to good words, the best of which are the words of Allah and remembrance of Him ﷻ, followed by supplications, sending blessings upon the Prophet ﷺ, and the stories of the Prophets, the Companions, the Followers, and the righteous. They soften the believer's heart, bring him peace, inspire him to be steadfast, and deepen his faith.

Imam al-Junayd al-Baghdādī (may Allah have mercy on him) said,

"The stories of the righteous are Allah's soldiers that He sends to the hearts." Indeed, we read many such stories in the Quran. Allah ﷻ even named one of the Sūras of the Quran *"Al-Qaṣaṣ"* [The Stories], and He tells us how these stories benefit us, **"And We relate to you ˹O Prophet˺ the stories of the Messengers to strengthen your heart."** [Quran 11:120] And, **"In their stories there truly is a lesson for people of understanding."** [Quran 12:111] Stories evoke praiseworthy sentiments in the believer's heart because they are in harmony with the faith that resides within.

On the other hand, when Allah ﷻ is mentioned, you might find disgust and aversion in the hearts of those who do not believe in Allah. He ﷻ said, **"Yet when Allah alone is mentioned, the hearts of those who disbelieve in the Hereafter are filled with disgust."** [Quran 39:45] Likewise, the disbelievers have an aversion to the stories of the Messengers and the righteous or to hearing someone engage in supplication.

What is portrayed in films and in stories shared on the news reveals the connection between a person's internal state and what he hears. True believers flee from evil statements and foul language because they maintain something of the pure and sound natural disposition (*fiṭra*) in which they were created.

These verses further elucidate this reality,

> **Indeed, there was a group of My servants who used to say, "Our Lord! We have believed, so forgive us and have mercy on us, for You are the best of those who show mercy." But you were ˹so busy˺ mocking them that it made you forget My remembrance, and you used to laugh at them. Today I have indeed rewarded them for their perseverance, that they are certainly the triumphant.**
> [Quran 23:109–111]

The believers here were firm upon that statement and were not swayed by the mockery of the disbelievers. They triumphed after the decreed time for this life came to an end—which is short in relation to what comes next. Even if the previous peoples lived for a thousand years or more, their lives were short in comparison to the Hereafter. Allah ﷻ has said, **"He will ask ⌜them⌝, 'How many years did you remain on earth?' They will reply, 'We remained ⌜only⌝ a day or part of a day, but ask those who kept count.' He will say, 'You only remained for a little while, if only you knew.'"** [Quran 23:112–114]

ANALYZING ONE'S STATE & ORIENTATION

Let us contemplate Allah's Words ﷻ, **"Those who believe and whose hearts find comfort in the remembrance of Allah. Surely in the remembrance of Allah do hearts find comfort."** [Quran 13:28] And, **"The ⌜true⌝ believers are only those whose hearts tremble at the remembrance of Allah, whose faith increases when His revelations are recited to them, and who put their trust in their Lord."** [Quran 8:2]

Look deeply within yourself and ask: what makes you happy and puts you at ease? What kinds of words? What kinds of stories? The answer reflects the harmony between your internal state, your orientation, and what types of things bring you comfort and joy when you hear them. Unfortunately, many people do not ask themselves these questions.

We need to nurture the hearts of our families and friends so that they find comfort and peace in the remembrance of Allah ﷻ and in the stories of the righteous. Enrich your life with this immense good; it causes your Lord's mercy to shower upon you, increases your understanding of religion, softens your heart, and has many other great benefits.

Many verses point to the immense significance of speech in the sight of Allah ﷻ. When highlighting the qualities of those He loves, Allah ﷻ often mentions their words, such as the following supplication, **"And those who *say*, 'Our Lord! Bless us with spouses and offspring who will be the joy of our hearts, and make us models for the righteous.'"** [Quran 25:74]

And He ﷻ said,

> **There are some who say, 'Our Lord! Grant us ˹Your bounties˺ in this world,' but they will have no share in the Hereafter. Yet there are others who say, 'Our Lord! Grant us the good of this world and the Hereafter, and protect us from the torment of the Fire.' It is they who will receive a ˹heavenly˺ reward for the good they have done. Surely Allah is swift in reckoning.** [Quran 2:200–202]

In these last two verses, Allah ﷻ describes the states of the two groups not based on their actions, but on their statements, "**There are some who *say*, 'Our Lord! Grant us ˹Your bounties˺ in this world,' but they will have no share in the Hereafter.**" Thus, if one turns to Allah in supplication and only asks for bodily health, abundant wealth, and material things, he misses out on his portion of the Hereafter, which is far greater.

"**Yet there are others who *say*, 'Our Lord! Grant us the good of this world and the Hereafter, and protect us from the torment of the Fire.' It is they who will receive a ˹heavenly˺ reward for the good they have done. Surely Allah is swift in reckoning.**" There are wondrous meanings in these verses. These statements represent the entirety of the heart's states and the outward deeds that are consistent with them. A Muslim should never underestimate the impact of the words that he utters nor of the words his heart finds comfort in.

We ask Allah ﷻ to turn our hearts constantly to Him. May He grant us excellent speech that allows us to receive the greatest amount of good in both worlds. May Allah's peace and blessings be upon our master Muhammad, and upon his Family and Companions. And all praise belongs to Allah, Lord of the Worlds.

CHAPTER 22

Beautiful Etiquettes of Giving & Receiving

All praise belongs to Allah, a praise that is perfect in every state. May Allah's peace and blessings be upon His servant, the Chosen One, the possessor of brilliantly shining light—and upon his Family which is the noblest of families, his Companions, and those who follow his path until the Last Day.

To proceed: The obligatory act of paying *zakāt* is crucial in overcoming the greed and selfishness of the lower self. This act relates to the heart and body. Allah ﷻ says, **"And whoever is saved from the selfishness of their own souls, it is they who are ˹truly˺ successful."** [Quran 59:9] The Prophet ﷺ said, *"Whoever possesses three qualities will be saved from the selfishness of his lower self: offering* zakāt, *honoring guests, and giving during times of hardship."*[112]

Zakāt, one of the five pillars of Islam, became obligatory in the 2nd year after the Hijra, and is applied to specific types of wealth. This is different from *zakāt al-fiṭr*, which must be paid at the end of Ramadan by every eligible individual, or it must be paid on their behalf by the person who supports them.

112 Narrated by al-Ṭabarānī in *al-Kabīr* on the authority of Zayd ibn Ḥāritha.

DONATING IS A SIGN OF FAITH

The extent to which a person is willing to give is according to the depth of their faith. Allah ﷻ made all kinds of wealth and worldly possessions beloved to the lower self. He then made giving away that very thing that it is in your nature to love a genuine sign of loving Him ﷻ. He has said ﷻ, **"You will never achieve righteousness until you give out some of what you cherish."** [Quran 3:92] Noble people compete in generosity, open-handedness, and donating.

Imam 'Abd al-Raḥmān ibn 'Abd-Allāh Bilfaqīh describes the exemplar of open-handedness and generosity, the Prophet Muhammad ﷺ:

> In generosity, he is like the overflowing ocean,
> He would give hundreds and thousands to those present,
> Yet he never chose or stored anything for himself,
> Except a little—and he had dependents to care for

He ﷺ once gave a man livestock that filled an entire valley. When the man returned to his people, he said to them, "My people, enter Islam! Truly, Muhammad gives as one who has no fear of poverty!"[113]

The key to donating (whether it be *zakāt*, voluntary charity, or a gift) is that we do it gladly and willingly, thereby reaping great blessings and reward. The great Companion Sa'd ibn Mu'ādh ؓ demonstrated this when he said to the Prophet ﷺ, "Take what you wish from our wealth, and leave for us whatever you please. What you take is more beloved to us than what you leave behind."[114]

The Companions were happy to give for Allah's sake ﷻ. Whatever was spent in supporting the cause of Allah and His Messenger was more beloved to them than anything that remained.

---

113 Narrated by Muslim in *Kitāb al-Faḍā'il* (Hadith 2312).

114 This was said during their expedition to the Battle of Badr when the Prophet consulted them about fighting the Quraysh.

THE PURPOSE OF WEALTH

It is essential to understand the true purpose of wealth. There are a range of perspectives on wealth. Some Muslims think that making money is an end in and of itself, losing their honor and resembling those who deny the ultimate return to Allah and the Final Abode.

Others make money only to fulfill their desires, which leads them to transgress the boundaries. They pay no attention to the fact that this approach will bring difficulty and tribulation, usually in this life before the next—and we seek refuge in Allah ﷻ. Others do not spend their money but hoard wealth for its own sake. People who care nothing for the Hereafter and make this world their only goal and concern will have a very difficult time when their souls leave their bodies. However, those who prepare for the Hereafter and are ready to meet their Lord will more likely have a favorable experience. They love to meet Allah, so Allah ﷻ loves to meet them.

The Noble Quran gives a clear description of the polytheists as those who neglect to give *zakāt*. Allah ﷻ says, **"And woe to the polytheists—those who do not pay the *zakāt*."** [Quran 41:6–7] This indicates that one's desire to hasten to give *zakāt* is according to the degree of his faith. Allah ﷻ mentions eight categories of *zakāt* recipients in the Quran, **"Alms-tax is only for the poor and the needy, for those employed to administer it, for those whose hearts are attracted ⌜to the faith⌝, for ⌜freeing⌝ slaves, for those in debt, for Allah's cause, and for ⌜needy⌝ travelers."** [Quran 9:60]

We must distribute our *zakāt* properly by giving it to eligible recipients. There are many Muslim businessmen who actively seek out people who are eligible to receive *zakāt*. Some fall prey to the devil's deception and give it to those who are not eligible, seeking their love and praise. If they fail to give their *zakāt* to eligible recipients, it is as if they never gave it and they are at fault.

Zakāt is an obligation to Allah ﷻ and it must be given to those specified by Him in His Book. It is an obligation to give *zakāt* completely and wholeheartedly so that it becomes a means of purification for the giver. The Prophet ﷺ said, emphasizing the benefits of *zakāt al-fiṭr*, *"It is a purification for the fasting person from falsehood and vulgar speech."*[115] In other words, it compensates for any defects and shortcomings in a person's fast, ensuring its acceptance by Allah ﷻ. Additionally, it is an obligation for people to take care of the poor and indigent locally so that they do not have to ask others for anything on Eid.

ATTAINING LOFTY DEGREES THROUGH INTENTIONS

How can we train our lower selves to give willingly? We need to reflect on the profound impact and reward of giving for the sake of Allah with complete sincerity. Allah ﷻ says, in praise of His pious and elect servants, **"They give food—out of love—to the poor, the orphan, and the captive, ˹saying,˺ 'We feed you only for the sake of Allah, seeking neither reward nor thanks from you. We fear from our Lord a horribly distressful Day.'"** [Quran 76:8–10]

The scholars of *Tafsīr* say that **"out of love"** carries two meanings. The first meaning is that **"love"** here signifies 'need,' indicating that they give despite their *own need* for the food.

The second meaning, which is greater and more sublime, is that **"out of love"** means 'out of love for Allah ﷻ.'[116] Our masters ʿAlī and Fāṭima ؉ exemplified this and acted out of love for Allah. They affirmed Him as their Lord and had certainty in their final return to Him. Out of their love for Allah, they generously provided food to a poor person, an orphan, and a captive. **"We feed you only for the sake of Allah,"** the One Whom

---

115 Narrated by Abū Dawūd in *Kitāb al-Zakāt* (Hadith 1609) and Ibn Māja in *Kitāb al-Zakāt*

116 Both meanings have been mentioned by Ibn Kathīr and al-Thaʿlabī in their respective *Tafsīr* works on this verse.

we love, and we express our love for Him by giving away what the lower self loves, hoping to receive Allah's good pleasure ﷻ.

The lofty degrees given to those who spend in Allah's cause depends on the loftiness of their aims, their inward purity, and their sincerity in seeking Allah's Noble Countenance ﷻ. The Prophet ﷺ said, *"One dirham surpassed one-hundred thousand dirhams."* He was then asked, "O Messenger of Allah, how can one dirham surpass one-hundred thousand?" He explained, *"A man ⌜only⌝ has two dirhams, and he takes one of them and gives it in charity. Another man has abundant wealth, and he takes one-hundred thousand dirhams from any part of it and gives it ⌜effortlessly⌝ in charity."*[117]

He described the way that the possessor of vast wealth, in giving one-hundred thousand dirhams, gives only a small portion in comparison to the rest of his wealth. Meanwhile, the giver of one dirham gives away half of his wealth. This is one reason why his charity surpassed the other's. The other reason is that whenever one's intention is more sincere and his heart is purer, the action is considered greater in the sight of Allah ﷻ.

When we physically give charity, we must be aware in our hearts that we are not doing the recipient a favor. The true Owner of the wealth is Allah. The Granter of Success is Allah. The One who entrusted it to us and subjugated our hearts to want to give is Allah ﷻ. The Creator of what was given and the One who facilitated its acceptance is Allah. It all belongs to Allah ﷻ. Thus, if the person who gives charity reminds the recipient of the favor, he becomes one of those whom Allah ﷻ does not gaze upon nor purifies on the Day of Resurrection. He receives a painful torment because he forgot the rights of the One who truly deserves recognition: Allah ﷻ.[118] Such a person seeks to establish himself as the

117 Narrated by al-Nasāʾī on the authority of Abū Dharr, and by Ibn Ḥibbān in his *Ṣaḥīḥ,* and al-Ḥākim in *al-Mustadrak* on the authority of Abū Hurayra.

118 This is an indication to the Hadith narrated by Muslim on the authority of Abū Dharr ؓ, who said that the Messenger of Allah ﷺ said, *"There are three types of people whom Allah does not speak to on the Day of Resurrection, nor does He gaze upon them or purify*

owner, the sustainer, the one in control, and the one who benefits and harms! He did not realize that Allah is the One who subjugated him to perform that action, and He subjugated other things for him as a test. Everything, in reality, belongs to Allah. He said ﷿, **"To Allah ⸢alone⸣ belongs the kingdom of the heavens and the earth."** [Quran 24:42]

Also, **"To Allah ⸢alone⸣ belongs all that is in the heavens and all that is on the earth."** [Quran 2:284]

And, **"All that is in the heavens and all that is on the earth glorifies Allah, for He is the Almighty, All-Wise."** [Quran 59:1]

We must strive to give from our wealth out of love for Allah ﷿. We should seek to reach the rank of those who prefer others over themselves as indicated in Allah's Words ﷿, **"They give preference over themselves even though they may be in need. And whoever is saved from the selfishness of their own souls, it is they who are ⸢truly⸣ successful."** [Quran 59:9] And He has said ﷿, **"They ⸢each⸣ have varying degrees in the sight of Allah. And Allah is All-Seeing of what they do."** [Quran 3:163]

THE ETIQUETTE OF RECEIVING CHARITY

People vary when it comes to their etiquette in receiving charity. A recipient of charity is judged based on his intention, aim, and heart's inclination. He must witness, in reality, that Allah is the Giver. Additionally, he must not take charity to amass more or to fulfill lowly desires. He cannot be dishonest about his true condition to receive charity. By being mindful of these principles, what he receives will be blessed and, when used properly, will produce positive outcomes.

One who is overly greedy and attached to the charity he receives will

---

them—and they receive a painful torment." He said that the Messenger of Allah ﷺ repeated this statement three times. Abū Dharr then responded, "They have failed and lost! Who are they, O Messenger of Allah?" He replied, *"The one ⸢whose lower garment⸣ drags on the ground, the one who reminds ⸢recipients⸣ of the favor ⸢of charity⸣, and the one who sells his merchandise falsely swearing by Allah."*

not find blessing in it. This is a principle that the Messenger of Allah ﷺ taught ʿUmar ibn al-Khaṭṭāb ؓ when he offered him some money. ʿUmar said, "Give it to someone who is more in need than I am." The Prophet ﷺ then said, *"Take it and accept it, then give it in charity. Whatever wealth comes to you that you are neither seeking nor asking for, then take it. If it is otherwise, then do not let your lower self desire it."*[119] The principle is that we do not let our lower selves desire or become attached to people's possessions. Another Hadith states, *"Whenever a person opens for himself the door of asking from people, Allah opens for him a door of poverty."*[120] The implications of poverty continue to grow within his heart, exhausting him and those around him. His life becomes difficult, and he receives a woeful compensation in the Hereafter.

We must therefore attach our hearts to Allah ﷻ so that both the one giving and the one receiving seek His good pleasure. When this is achieved, societies become rectified, benefit and goodness spread, and calamities are warded off. The Hadith states, *"Truly, charity given in secret extinguishes the Lord's anger and wards off a tragic death."*[121]

O Allah, make us those who are true, charitable, sincere, giving, and who seek Your forgiveness at the end of the night—by Your mercy, O Most Merciful. May Allah's peace and blessings be upon our master Muhammad, and upon his Family and Companions. All praise belongs to Allah, Lord of the Worlds.

---

119 Narrated by al-Bukhārī in *Kitāb al-Aḥkām* (Hadith 67), Muslim in *Kitāb al-Zakāt* (Hadith 1040), al-Nasāʾī, and Aḥmad on the authority of ʿUmar ibn al-Khaṭṭāb.

120 Narrated by Imam Aḥmad in *al-Musnad*.

121 Narrated by al-Ṭabarānī in *al-Awsaṭ*.

CHAPTER 23

Supplications & True Honor

All praise belongs to Allah, the All-Merciful, the Most Merciful, the Sovereign, the Most Generous. We ask Him to bestow the best and purest of peace and blessings upon His Chosen Servant, the possessor of magnificent character—and upon his Family, Companions, and all who follow his upright way.

To proceed: Among the things that impact the Kingdom of the Heart are the supplications that we choose. The Companions would often request certain supplications from the Messenger of Allah ﷺ and Allah ﷻ gifted us supplications in His Mighty Book and taught us to use them to call on Him. As mentioned previously, Allah ﷻ praised those who supplicate Him by saying, **"Our Lord! Grant us the good of this world and the Hereafter, and protect us from the torment of the Fire."** [Quran 2:201] An authentic Hadith states that the Prophet ﷺ used to repeat this *duʿā* abundantly.

THE GREATEST MIRACLE IS UPRIGHTNESS

One of the most profound supplications that Allah teaches us is found in the Fātiḥa, the greatest Sūra of the Quran: **"Guide us to the Straight Path, the Path of those You have blessed."** [Quran 1:6–7] Guidance on the Straight Path is the greatest thing we can seek from Allah ﷻ since He called us to remain steadfast upon it. When we ask Him for His enabling grace (*tawfiq*) and assistance in doing what He called us to, the value of the request is immense. We ask Him to establish all the qualities within us that He called us to adorn ourselves with, and that He rid us of all the qualities that He warned us against and forbade us from. This is why one of the pious predecessors said, "Uprightness is the greatest miracle."

One of the highest honors Allah ﷻ gives to a servant is that He grants him the enabling grace to be upright in his words, actions, and states. Although Allah may allow an extraordinary occurrence to happen to someone, such as walking on water, this could be a genuine miracle of divine favor (*karāma*) or it could be what is called *istidrāj*, which deludes that person and steers him even further from the truth.

The lower self is mesmerized by extraordinary occurrences, and there are some who wrongly associate *wilāya* and nearness to Allah ﷻ based on them occurring at someone's hands.[122] This is not the case. Many of Allah's servants never experience these miraculous events and yet are higher in rank than some of those who do. The people of Allah say, "Being in a complete state of presence with Allah in one *rak'a* of Prayer is better than manifesting seventy miracles."

The desire to perform miracles stems from the lower self. Sincere worshippers strive to rid their hearts of this desire. Their only objective is to respond to Allah's command with exaltation and glorification of Him, establish the rights of His Lordship, and actualize their servitude to Him ﷻ. They remain vigilant against being influenced by the whims of their passion. Scholars who are firmly rooted in knowledge and the *awliyā'* are the furthest people from succumbing to their lower desires and

---

122 Translator's note: *Wilāya* is the state of close proximity to Allah ﷻ. The person who is granted this is called a *walī* (plural: *awliyā'*). See Quran 2:257 and 10:62; and al-Bukhārī in *Kitāb al-Riqāq* (Hadith 6502).

are extremely wary of this. Most miracles of divine favor that manifest at their hands occur without their desire or conscious attention to them, occurring either spontaneously or out of necessity.

We see this clearly in the life of the Prophet Muhammad ﷺ: how many difficult circumstances did he patiently bear? How many periods of hunger and thirst did he endure? In most instances, the Prophet exercised patience. Yet in other situations, for a specific wisdom, he performed miracles. Prophets are commanded to perform miracles to call people to Allah, to establish the proof of their truthfulness, and to open the doors of Allah's mercy for His creation ﷻ.

You must understand that the true miracle of divine favor is to become adorned with the qualities that are beloved to Allah and to be purified from disobeying Him ﷻ. Scholars consider the basis and measure of a person's uprightness his adhering to and following the Sunna of the Chosen One ﷺ. It is incorrect to think that a person who has a greater degree of *wilāya* with Allah necessarily manifests more extraordinary acts. A breaking of the norm could be a divine favor for a righteous servant, which then only increases him in humility and good manners with Allah ﷻ. On the other hand, the extraordinary act could be trickery and deception, either sorcery or sleight of hand for those who engage in such practices.

THE DAJJĀL'S MIRACLES OF DELUSION

Another type of extraordinary act occurs when Allah ﷻ humiliates some of His enemies by making extraordinary things happen contrary to the outcome that evil person seeks. Or the occurrence could be a miracle of delusion (*istidrāj*), breaking the norm in a manner that the disbeliever *does* desire—which occurs with the Dajjāl at the end of time.

Every Prophet warned his community of the Dajjāl, and our Prophet ﷺ warned us of him as well and gave us additional insight that was not mentioned by the Prophets before him. He said ﷺ, *"Whatever is unclear to you about him, then let it be clear that your Lord is not one-eyed, whereas he* (i.e., the Dajjāl) *is one-eyed."* Therefore, do not be deceived by the miracles of delusion that the Dajjāl manifests at the end of time.

It has been narrated in the two *Ṣaḥīḥ* collections that one of the best of those killed in Allah's cause is a person who is killed by the Dajjāl and then brought back to life by him outside of Madina. The Dajjāl invites this young man to believe in him, but the man says, "You are the one-eyed Dajjāl, the liar, who the Messenger of Allah informed us of!" The Dajjāl then cuts him in half and walks between the two halves of his separated body. Then the Dajjāl says, "Arise!" after which the man comes back to life, by Allah's will, as a test for the believers.

When the man stands up, the Dajjāl asks, "Do you believe in me?" He replies, "Now I am even more aware of who you are. O people, he will not be able to do anything to anyone after me!" Then the Dajjāl takes hold of the man to kill him, but the area between the man's neck and collarbone becomes copper, so the Dajjāl is completely unable to harm him or anyone after him for the time that remains of his tribulation, which surges throughout the earth.[123] People become ensnared in this test because of their desires. When these desires take over, they make people abandon their principles and good character. So beware of this.

The believers seek refuge in the mountains where they endure hunger until Allah ﷻ sends female gazelles whose milk sustains them. Others are nourished by repeatedly saying *'Subḥān Allāh'* [Glory belongs to Allah] until the days of the Dajjāl come to an end. It is narrated in a Hadith that after Jesus's descent ﵇, he informs those who were steadfast during the time of the Dajjāl of their places in Paradise. Their being informed of this is a reward for their patient perseverance. This helps

---

123 The story is found in the two *Ṣaḥīḥ* books: al-Bukhari in *Kitāb al-Fitan* (Hadith 6713) and Muslim in *Kitāb al-Fitan* (Hadith 2938).

us understand how success is attained through patience and teaches us the importance of asking Allah ﷻ for guidance.

PROPHETIC SUPPLICATIONS

Returning to our initial discussion on the importance of choosing supplications, let us now consider the supplications that the Companions requested from the Prophet ﷺ. The Prophet's wife ʿAisha ﵂ asked, "O Messenger of Allah, if I find that it is *Laylat al-Qadr*, what supplication should I make?" He replied ﷺ, *"Say: Allāhumma innaka ʿafūwwun tuḥibbu'l ʿafwa, faʿfu ʿannī"* [O Allah, You are Pardoning and You love to pardon, so grant me Your pardon]. He taught her this comprehensive and exalted *duʿā* by which she could seek her Generous Lord's pardon—and He ﷻ is excellent in His pardoning. When Allah pardons and forgives, He conceals His servants' mistakes, becomes the guarantor of the wrongs they have committed against others, causes the one wronged to forgive him, and He enters them into Paradise by His mercy.

It is essential to regularly recite Quranic supplications as well as those passed down from the Prophet ﷺ. One supplication that we should always make is the supplication for the end of gatherings. The Prophet ﷺ taught us to conclude our gatherings with a supplication that would atone for any wrongs and preserve any good that took place during the gathering. He taught us to say as we rise from the gathering, *"Subḥānak Allāhumma wa bi ḥamdik, ashhadu an lā ilāha illā anta, astaghfiruka wa atūbu ilayk"* [Glorious are You, O Allah, and praise belongs to You. I bear witness that there is no god except You. I seek Your forgiveness and turn to You in repentance].[124]

The Prophet ﷺ also taught us to say as we leave the house, *"Bismillāh, tawakkaltu ʿalā Allāh, wa lā ḥawla wa lā quwwata illā billāh"* [In the

124 Narrated by Aḥmad, al-Tirmidhī who classified it as a *ḥasan gharīb saḥīḥ,* Abū Dawūd, and al-Nasāʾī.

Name of Allah, I place my trust in Allah, and there is no power nor ability except by Allah]. Whenever someone says these words when leaving the house, an angel responds with, "You are guided, sufficed, and protected." The devil assigned to him is distanced, and another devil says to the first, "What can you do to a man who is guided, sufficed, and protected?"[125]

Before going to sleep, the Prophet ﷺ taught us to say *"Subḥān Allāh"* thirty-three times, *"Al-ḥamdu lillāh"* thirty-three times, and *"Allāhu Akbar"* thirty-three or thirty-four times. Doing this is more helpful than having a servant, as the Prophet ﷺ taught his dear daughter Fāṭima al-Zahrā' and son-in-law 'Alī ؓ. When they asked him for a servant, he taught them these supplications instead.[126]

This teaches us to select words and supplications that are a means for provisions, that open doors of divine goodness, and that protect us from evil. The great Companion Ḥudhayfa ibn al-Yamān ؓ said, "A time will come when the only one saved is a person who supplicates like someone who is drowning."[127]

O Allah, make us people who supplicate, whose prayers are accepted, and whose requests are answered—O Lord of the Worlds! May Allah's peace and blessings be upon our master Muhammad, and upon his Family and Companions. All praise belongs to Allah, Lord of the Worlds.

125 Narrated by al-Tirmidhī who classified it as *ḥasan ṣaḥīḥ*, and by Abū Dawūd (the wording above is taken from his narration).

126 Narrated by al-Bukhārī in *Kitāb al-Nafaqāt* (Hadith 5046) and Muslim in *Kitāb al-Dhikr wa'l Du'ā wa'l Tawba wa'l Istighfār* (Hadith 2727).

127 Narrated by al-Ḥākim.

CHAPTER 24

Studying the Life of the Prophet ﷺ

All praise belongs to Allah, the Sovereign, the Opener, the All-Knowing, the Bountiful, the Munificent, the Most Generous. There is no god except Him, One without partner. He sent His Chosen Servant to us, Muhammad, making him the Seal of His Messengers. He honored him by revealing to him the Wise Reminder. O Allah, send peace and blessings upon our master Muhammad, his pure Family, his elect Companions, and upon those who follow his path, and include us with them and among them, by Your mercy, O Most Merciful.

To proceed: Studying the lives of the Prophets ﷺ has an extremely powerful impact on the heart. It connects us to the realities of prophethood and to the One who taught the Prophets and Messengers. Our Lord mentions the stories of the Messengers in the Quran and these stories contain immense benefits. Therefore, we must have the utmost devotion to the stories of the Master of Messengers and the Seal of the Prophets, our master Muhammad ﷺ, their Imam and leader.

Studying the Prophetic biography (*al-Sīra al-Nabawīyya*) is very effective in purifying the heart, is filled with benefit, and has a profound impact on bringing relief to one's heart. Studying his life ﷺ connects us all with our exemplar, role model, and locus of Allah's good pleasure ﷺ, so that we take him as a leader and are guided by him.

LESSONS FROM THE CONQUEST OF MECCA

The Conquest of Mecca, which occurred during the last ten days of Ramadan, teaches us many lessons that we as an Ummah need to reflect upon. Let us assess our current state and what stories shape our thoughts. Certain stories may negatively influence us, especially if their protagonists are people who brazenly disobey Allah ﷻ and even ridicule obedience to Him and worship of Him.

Since stories have an immense impact in shaping our thoughts, we must be mindful of what stories we allow to shape our minds and those of our families and friends. Acknowledging that our friends, those in our care, and our neighbors have rights over us is a fundamental aspect of human dignity and faith. The Quran emphasizes this when Allah ﷻ addresses the believers, saying, **"O believers! Protect yourselves and your families from a Fire whose fuel is people and stones. . ."** [Quran 66:6] And, **"O believers! Indeed, some of your spouses and children are enemies to you, so beware of them."** [Quran 64:14]

He ﷻ also said, **"And know that your wealth and your children are only a test, and that with Allah is a great reward."** [Quran 8:28] The Prophet Muhammad ﷺ also said, *"By Allah, the one whose neighbor is not safe from his harm is not a believer."*[128]

The believers are advised to be mindful of the company they keep and of the content they allow to saturate their thoughts and minds. People will find nothing more beneficial for the mind than what Allah ﷻ—the Creator and One to Whom we return—is pleased with. Allah ﷻ revealed His Book and sent His Chosen One only to infuse our minds, thoughts, and hearts with the light found in it and in the radiant Sunna. Therefore, it is essential to remind one another of these stories.

Unfortunately, many of our children do not even know the year or month when the Conquest of Mecca took place, which occurred in the

128 Narrated by al-Bukhārī in *Kitāb al-Adab* (Hadith 5670) and Muslim in *Kitāb al-Īmān* (Hadith 46) on the authority of Abū Shurayḥ.

month of Ramadan in the 8th year after the Hijra. The Prophet ﷺ entered Mecca during the last ten days of Ramadan, conquering it after enduring patiently for many years, bearing great hardship, and overcoming many difficulties. Throughout it all, he remained in a state of contentment, tranquility, and submission to Allah. In the years before the Hijra, the Prophet ﷺ faced unspeakable harm in Mecca—he was ridiculed, insulted, choked, had thorns placed in his path, and more.

In the 6th year after the Hijra, the Prophet ﷺ set out to perform the 'Umrah, the minor pilgrimage. Before the Prophet ﷺ entered Mecca, his camel Qaṣwā' kneeled and refused to rise. The Companions said, "Qaṣwā' is being stubborn!" The Messenger ﷺ replied, *"Qaṣwā' is not being stubborn—that is not her character. Rather, she has been held back by the One who held back the elephant."*

He then said, regarding negotiations with the people of Mecca at Ḥudaybīa, *"By the One in whose hand lies my soul, were they to request anything from me in return for revering what Allah has made inviolable, I would surely grant them it."*[129] He exemplified the sublime character that is needed to truly rise above worldly conflicts. The phrase, 'the battle between truth and falsehood' is used by many people, but the Prophet ﷺ truly embodied its meaning. He set out to guide people to Allah, call to Him, resist evil, and ward off oppression and tyranny. His sublime behavior rises above mere disputation and does not at all resemble, much less imitate, the people of falsehood.

This is why he ﷺ said, after the Battle of Uḥud, *"We are not equal. Our dead are in Paradise and your dead are in the Fire."*[130] This is not an empty claim, nor is it the case for every Muslim in every context. Rather, it applies to those who become spiritually purified of blameworthy qualities.

---

129 Narrated by al-Bukhārī in *Kitāb al-Shurūṭ* (Hadith 2581).

130 The Prophet ﷺ said this in response to Abū Sufyān when he said, after the Battle of Uḥud, "This day makes us even for the Day of Badr. Victory alternates and war is a competition." Narrated by Aḥmad and al-Ḥākim in *al-Mustadrak* on the authority of 'Umar—and he said its chain of transmission is authentic.

During the Conquest of Mecca, when Allah granted the Muslims victory over those who opposed the Prophet from the beginning of his mission and harmed him and his Companions for many years, the Prophet was not the least bit influenced by the worldly notions that preoccupy most people's minds at such moments.

When some of the noble Companions thought that the way to demonstrate the triumph of belief over disbelief was to humiliate the disbelievers, the Messenger corrected them and did something far more effective instead.

On the day when Allah honored His Messenger and allowed him to conquer Mecca, the Prophet commanded his uncle al-ʿAbbās to remain at the entry point to the city with Abū Sufyān, who at that time was the leader of the disbelievers. Abū Sufyān was watching as the army passed by, and when Saʿd ibn ʿUbāda passed him, he said, "Abū Sufyān, today is the day of slaughter. Today is the day when it will be permissible to shed blood around the Kaʿba. Today is the day that Allah will abase Quraysh." Naturally, Abū Sufyān was disturbed by what he had heard.

He informed the Prophet of what Saʿd had said, so the Prophet corrected the statement and clarified what that day really represented. He said, *"Rather, today is the day of mercy. Today is the day the Kaʿba will be adorned. Today is the day Allah will honor Quraysh."*[131] This notion was deeply rooted within him before the Conquest of Mecca—indeed, even before he left Mecca to migrate to Madina. Early on in his mission, when ʿUthmān ibn Abū Ṭalḥa prevented the Prophet from entering the Kaʿba because the leaders of Quraysh were inside, he said to him, *"ʿUthmān, perhaps you will one day see the key ⌜to the Kaʿba⌝ in my hands giving it to whomever I please."* ʿUthmān countered, "Then on that day Quraysh will be ruined and humiliated!" To which the Prophet said, *"Rather, they will be prosperous and honored on that day."*[132]

131 Narrated by al-Bukhārī in *Kitāb al-Maghāzī* (Hadith 4030).

132 Narrated by Ibn Saʿd in *al-Ṭabaqāt*.

The Prophet's principles never changed. He never thought to humiliate anyone or violate their rights. Rather, his concern was to spread honor and prosperity to all of humanity on earth through what Allah ﷻ had revealed to him. It is therefore necessary that our notions be governed by these understandings as well.

When Abū Sufyān saw the strength of the Muslim army, he asked, "Who are these people, 'Abbās?" Al-'Abbās answered, "The Messenger of Allah ﷺ and the Migrants and Helpers." He replied, "By Allah, your nephew has become a great king!" Al-'Abbās immediately corrected his understanding, and said, "It is not kingship. Rather, it is Prophethood." Abū Sufyān then said, "Then this is certainly good."

Most people desire power and influence, but the Prophet ﷺ taught us that these desires have no place in the religion and are never sought by people who are true with Allah ﷻ. At the beginning of his mission, he ﷺ was offered to become the ruler of Mecca on the condition that he leave some of what he was commanded to convey, but he rejected their offer. Yet, some people today come up with far-off notions, saying, "By becoming a ruler, I can eventually establish Allah's commands, even if it takes me a long time." The Prophet ﷺ refused to reign from the very beginning, guided by true insight and realization.

CORRECTING NOTIONS OF WORLDLY POWER

One of the current deficiencies among Muslims is that their minds and thoughts have been infiltrated by ideas that cause them to act like the disbelievers. Although Muslims might adopt similar outward means as disbelievers, their aims must be exalted. They cannot compromise their principles at all.

Let us reflect on people's notions of the caliphate that the Messenger of Allah ﷺ promised would be established on the earth at the end of time. Being happy with this caliphate should not be based on one's hope for worldly gains or because one's group has authority. These are misunderstandings that plague many people. Being happy with the fulfillment of this promise is only due to the mercy that Allah's servants receive, the rectification of their affairs and uprightness, and the preeminence and manifestation of the truth. These are what every person who is sincere with Allah ﷻ hopes for.

On the other hand, some people's lower selves become attached to the abundant wealth that becomes widespread at that time. We are told that there will be so much prosperity that people will be unable to find anyone in need of charity. Such a person's heart gets attached to these aspects, as if his only wish in this worldly life is to eat and drink. However, he can find similar provisions with the Dajjāl—will he be pleased with that? Would he like to join him? This matter holds far greater significance.

We say: being pleased with Allah's gifts and properly setting out in the path of Allah ﷻ to manifest those gifts for people cannot be done to give authority to fleeting and transient desires. Rather, truly setting out in the path of Allah is achieved through purification of the heart and making one's intentions and actions solely for Allah ﷻ. Not every person who claims to support the cause of Allah is actually doing so. Many people are actually calling others to themselves despite their belief that they are calling to Allah ﷻ.

I ask Allah the Most Generous to take care of and rectify our affairs, alleviate the calamities of the people of Islam, purify their hearts, and prepare them for the manifestation of good for them and within them. May Allah's peace and blessings be upon our master Muhammad, his Family, and Companions. All praise belongs to Allah, Lord of the Worlds.

CHAPTER 25

Basing Our Interactions on Prophetic Guidance

All praise belongs to Allah, our Generous Lord. May Allah's peace and blessings be upon His Prophet, the compassionate and merciful, and upon his Family and Companions, and upon those who follow his upright way.

To proceed: In the previous chapter, we learned some lessons from the Prophet's interactions with his friends and foes at the Conquest of Mecca. We discussed how he ﷺ corrected the words used by Sa'd ibn 'Ubāda ؓ. He changed, "day of slaughter" to *"day of mercy,"* and "blood will be shed at the Ka'ba" to *"the Ka'ba will be adorned,"* and "Allah will abase Quraysh" to *"Allah will honor Quraysh."*

THE PROPHET'S MAGNIFICENT CHARACTER ﷺ

Consider the notion of wanting to honor those whose homes and lands were conquered, not abase them. This is because the Prophet's principles are far above the whims and misconceptions that dominate people's minds. Allah ﷻ tells us, **"If you were to obey most of those on earth, they would lead you away from Allah's way. They follow nothing but assumptions and do nothing but lie."** [Quran 6:116]

But Allah's Beloved ﷺ is different. Allah ﷻ attests to the truthfulness of his speech, **"He does not speak of his own whims. It is only a revelation sent down ˹to him˺."** [Quran 53:3–4]

The people of Mecca had tried their utmost to stand in the way of Allah's religion and fought against His people. The Prophet's intention ﷺ was to help them abandon their evil ways so that they could be taken from disgrace to true nobility and honor. They were people who followed their lower selves, their whims, and the devil, and this made them distant from Allah ﷻ. The Prophet ﷺ helped them to become true servants of their Creator. They were on the brink of entering the Fire, but he then showed them the path to everlasting bliss in the Garden. The Prophet ﷺ did this to elevate and honor them.

His followers must have that same concern in their hearts for all people, even those who wage war against them. They hope that Allah nevertheless grants the transgressors true nobility by changing their current state. They may be proud, arrogant, and seem to be in a position of strength, but the reality is that that they are in a humiliating state. Do those of us who wish to serve the truth and be true representatives of the Prophet ﷺ understand this? We will not succeed unless we have these prophetic qualities, a deep understanding of realities of this life and the next, and we sincerely seek Allah's good pleasure ﷻ.

We see these sublime meanings when the Prophet ﷺ entered Mecca. He forbade his Companions from fighting anyone except in self-defense. The only exception to this were the several people whose lives the Prophet ﷺ allowed to be taken due to the harm that they had done—although most of these people were eventually pardoned and forgiven.

He then emphasized the sanctity of Mecca, teaching the Companions that no matter how much aggressors fight against and harm us, we will not allow our lower selves to react impulsively. We will always revere what Allah ﷻ has made exalted. Although they revere the Holy Sanctuary in their own way, we do not let their enmity cause us to deny the inviolability of the Holy Sanctuary because it is Allah's House. Everything centers on seeking Allah's good pleasure ﷻ. Whoever's aim is such, he attains true glory, **"So whoever hopes for the meeting with their Lord, let him do good deeds and associate none in the worship of his Lord."** [Quran 18:110]

THE FOUNDATION FOR PEOPLE OF TRUTH

We cannot realize our servitude to Allah ﷻ and establish His commands according to our whims and limited understanding. We can only do this by freeing ourselves from the control of the lower self that commands to evil. **"And as for those who were in awe of standing before their Lord and restrained themselves from desires, Paradise will certainly be ⌜their⌝ home."** [Quran 79:40–41]

In this manner, Allah's deputyship ﷻ was established on the earth, first by Adam ﷺ and then by the Prophets and Messengers that came after him. It was perfected and completed in the Seal of Messengers, Muhammad ﷺ. He said, *"Truly, the likeness of me and the Prophets before me is that of a man who built a house. He adorned it and beautified it, except for one brick that was missing in a corner. People walked around ⌜the house⌝ and were in wonder, asking him, 'Why have you not laid this brick?' I am that brick, and I am the Seal of Prophets."*[133]

This distinction is what makes the people of truth have a completely different outlook than those who have gone astray. Their path of deviation takes them away from Muhammad, the way of Muhammad, belief in Muhammad, and following Muhammad ﷺ. He is the Seal of Prophets, and his Sacred Law abrogates all previous laws.

Understanding this helps us recognize some aspects of perfection in the objectives the Prophet ﷺ called us to. There are times when we

133 Narrated by al-Bukhārī in *Kitāb al-Manāqib* (Hadith 3324) and Muslim in *Kitāb al-Faḍā'il* (Hadith 2286).

show a certain firmness towards disbelievers, which is driven by noble intentions and has absolutely no association to the tendencies of the lower self. The Companions overcame their lower selves, so do not be amazed by their sublime behavior.

When fighting in Allah's cause, Imam 'Alī ﷺ defeated a disbeliever in battle. Before 'Alī ﷺ struck the final blow, the disbeliever spat in his face. 'Alī ﷺ immediately lowered his sword and did not strike him. When asked about what had occurred, he said, "When he spat in my face, I become angered for my own self and wanted to strike him out of vengeance—but I only strike with my sword for Allah's sake." These are the teachings he received from Muhammad ﷺ. We must strive to embody these teachings in our dealings and remain conscious of our exemplar ﷺ.

THE PROPHET'S SUBLIME INTERACTIONS ﷺ

When reflecting on the Conquest of Mecca, we witness the Prophet's noble principles, values, and etiquettes. Before the conquest, the Prophet ﷺ ordered the announcement to be made: "Whoever enters Abū Sufyān's house is safe! Whoever enters his own house and closes his door is safe! Whoever enters the Holy Sanctuary is safe!"[134]

He allowed Abū Sufyān's name to be called out, even though just days before, he was an enemy combatant. Recognizing Abū Sufyān's love to be held in high esteem, the Prophet ﷺ allowed for his name to be called out, aiming to bring him closer to Allah ﷻ, so that he could eventually be rid of the love of esteem and other diseases of the heart.

Following this, the Prophet ﷺ came to the Holy Sanctuary, destroyed the idols, entered the Ka'ba, and prayed inside of it. Afterwards, he came out and held onto the door of the Ka'ba. At this point, many members of Quraysh had gathered there. Despite having the power to kill, punish,

134 Narrated by Muslim in *Kitāb al-Jihād* (Hadith 1780).

and imprison any of the Meccans, he instead pronounced the statement of truth, *"There is no god but Allah, One without partner. He fulfilled His promise, gave victory to His servant, and He alone defeated the confederates."*

Imagine your Prophet ﷺ as he grasped the doors of the Ka'ba and recited this statement—a statement for which people opposed and persecuted him, leading to his migration from Mecca. On that day, he stood at the door of the Ka'ba and openly announced it. The people who used to harm him and his Companions were all around him, and he addressed them, *"O assembly of Quraysh, what do you think I am going to do with you?"* They replied, "Treat us well. You are a noble brother, the son of a noble brother." He said, *"You are all free to go."* He issued a general amnesty by which he pardoned all past offenses. People then understood the exaltedness of this man and of his way, and that he did not desire the world, sovereignty, or vengeance. One of the Quraysh said, "Only a Prophet could be so gracious."[135] After witnessing the beauty of the Prophet Muhammad's character ﷺ, people embraced Islam in great numbers.

Despite this, there remained a man, Fuḍāla ibn 'Umayr al-Laythī, who wanted to kill the Prophet ﷺ. As the Prophet ﷺ was circumambulating the Ka'ba, Fuḍāla was trailing behind him, waiting for the opportunity to stab the Prophet from behind. When Fuḍāla came close, the Prophet stopped and turned to him. He said, *"Are you Fuḍāla?"* He replied, "Yes." The Prophet ﷺ said, *"What were you just thinking to yourself?"* Fuḍāla said, "Nothing! I was only remembering Allah." The Messenger smiled. As the man stood before him, the Prophet could do whatever he wanted to him. Instead of retaliating, the Prophet ﷺ placed his hand on Fuḍāla's chest and prayed for him.

Fuḍāla said, "By Allah, by the time he lifted his hand, there was no

135 This was said by Ṣafwān ibn Umayya when he embraced Islam at Ḥunayn after the Prophet gave him a great amount of wealth from the spoils of war. [*Al-Iṣāba fī Tamyīz al-Ṣaḥāba*]

man on the face of the earth more beloved to me than him." Allah ﷻ cured him of those diseases, and he became a true lover of Allah and His Messenger ﷺ.

Fuḍāla proved to have exemplary etiquette with Allah and respect for the Sharia. Immediately after this interaction with the Prophet, he left the Holy Sanctuary. A woman he used to speak with called out to him, saying, "Come here and let's talk." Fuḍāla, now a changed man, replied,

> She said, 'Come here and let's talk,' so I said,
> 'No! Allah forbids you, as does Islam,'
> Had you seen Muhammad and his folk
> During the Conquest, the day the idols were destroyed,
> You would have seen Allah's religion emerge clearly
> And polytheism conceal its darkened façade[136]

May Allah's blessings be upon the possessor of light, magnanimity, and the most merciful, expansive, and compassionate heart. O Allah, make us firm upon his way, gather us in his company, and grant us the reality of giving victory to You and to him. May Allah's peace and blessings be upon our master Muhammad, his Family, and his Companions. Allah praise belongs to Allah, Lord of the Worlds.

136 Narrated by Ibn Hishām in the 5th volume of his *Sīra.* He also mentioned that the Conquest of Mecca occurred in the month of Ramadan in the 8th year after the Hijra.

CHAPTER 26

Respecting Differences of Opinion

All praise belongs to Allah, the Manifest, the Real. There is no god except Him, Master of the Day of Judgment. He sent His Servant to us, the Chosen One, the Trustworthy—Muhammad—with guidance and the religion of truth to make it prevail over all other religions, to the dismay of the polytheists. O Allah, send Your ceaseless peace and blessings on Your Servant Muhammad, the possessor of lofty degrees, and upon his Family, Companions, and all those who follow his way with steadfastness. May we be included with them and counted among them, O Answerer of prayers!

To proceed: Having a deep understanding of our servitude to Allah ﷻ and how we worship Him is one of the foundations of the Kingdom of the Heart that helps us remain steadfast. One element of this which merits thorough examination is understanding jurisprudence and how scholars arrive at legal judgments.

THE BREADTH OF THE SHARIA

The various legal schools were established based on sound juristic judgments from the Quran, Sunna, observance of consensus (*ijmāʿ*), and excellence in analogous reasoning (*qiyās*). They represent the Book and

Sunna's exaltedness and breadth. We need to understand the wisdom behind its breadth, as it allows people to practice and implement the Sacred Law and fulfill their varying needs in different times and places. Its expansiveness should teach us to have the proper etiquette with Allah ﷻ and be less narrow-minded, broadening our intellectual horizons. Those who have the competency required for legal reasoning should not raise their personal opinions to the level of the Word of Allah and His Messenger by making them undebatable. The life of the Prophet Muhammad ﷺ is filled with examples of these differences with respect to various acts of worship.

For example, when it comes to voluntary Prayers, we find that some people perform many prayers, and some perform fewer. A Hadith states, *"Prayer is the best prescribed act, so whoever desires, let him pray abundantly; and whoever desires, let him pray only a little."*[137] It is narrated that each night some of the eminent Companions would pray 20 *rak'as,* some would pray 30 *rak'as*, and some would pray 100 *rak'as* (such as 'Uthmān ibn 'Affān ﷺ), while others would pray less.

Additionally, the Companions would make a variety of supplications in their Prayers, with some supplicating out loud and having the Prophet ﷺ hear and validate them. In an authentic Hadith narrated by Ibn 'Umar ﷺ, he relates that, "While we were praying with the Messenger of Allah ﷺ, one of the men praying said, *'Allāhu Akbaru Kabīrā, wa'l ḥamdu lillāhi kathīrā, wa subḥān Allahi bukratan wa aṣīlā!'* [Allah is truly Great, all praise belongs to Him in abundance, and glory belongs to Allah morning and evening!] The Messenger of Allah ﷺ then asked, *'Who was it that said such-and-such?'* The man said, 'It was me, O Messenger of Allah.' The Prophet said, *'It amazed me—the gates of heaven opened for it.'*" Ibn 'Umar said, "I never abandoned these words ever since I heard

137 Narrated by Aḥmad, Ibn Ḥibbān, and al-Ḥākim who stated that it was authentic on the authority of Abū Dharr.

Allah's Messenger ﷺ say that."[138] He revered and cherished these words because the Prophet approved them and gave good news to the man who had uttered them.

It has been narrated in another authentic Hadith on the authority of Rifāʿa ibn Rāfiʿ (may Allah be pleased with him), who said, "One day, we were praying with Allah's Messenger ﷺ, and when he rose from the bowing position, he said, *'Samiʿ Allāhu liman ḥamida,'* [Allah hears those who praise Him] after which a man responded, *'Rabbanā wa laka al-ḥamd, ḥamdan kathīran ṭayyiban mubārakan fīh.'* [Our Lord, to You belongs all praise—abundant, pure, and blessed praise!] When the Messenger of Allah ﷺ completed the Prayer, he said, *'Who just spoke?'* The man said, 'It was me, O Messenger of Allah.' The Messenger of Allah ﷺ said, *'I saw thirty-odd angels racing to record it.'*"[139] He gave him the good news of the angels racing to write those words and to record the rewards for the person who said them. Since the Prophet's word is law ﷺ, his validating their supplications allowed for them to be recited in the Prayer.

RESPECTING DIFFERENCES OF OPINION

There are numerous examples of how the noble Companions called upon Allah (Exalted is He) using different supplications. When calling upon Allah, it is recommended to use the supplications found in the Quran and Sunna, although we are not limited to these alone. When we follow the teachings of the Prophet ﷺ, we will be rightly guided. He taught us that supplicating is encouraged, so long as it is not a request for something sinful, such as the severing of family ties.

The Prophet ﷺ would teach one Companion a certain supplication and a different supplication to another Companion—and at no point did

138 Narrated by Muslim in *Kitāb al-Masājid wa Mawaḍiʿ al-Ṣalā* (Hadith 150).

139 Narrated by Aḥmad, Abū Dawūd, al-Nasāʾī, and al-Ḥākim who said that its chain of narration is authentic. It was also narrated in al-Bukhārī and Muslim with a similar wording to this narration.

he obligate anyone to make only one supplication. It is also important to note that the Companions did not limit themselves to the supplications he had taught them to the rejection of all other supplications.

Our traveling the path to Allah ﷻ requires that we have pure hearts and excellent dealings with others. Therefore, we cannot be narrow-minded, force things that are not obligatory upon others, or condemn anyone for doing things that the Sunna approves (nor can we approve things that the Sunna forbids). We learn this from the way of the noble Companions ﷺ who experienced this breadth during the life of the Prophet ﷺ. One of the Companions narrates, "We went out with Allah's Messenger ﷺ from Minā to 'Arafāt. Some of us were saying the *talbīya*[140] while others were saying, *'Allāhu Akbar.'*"[141] As for the Prophet ﷺ, he adhered to the *talbīya* until he threw the stones at the *Jamarāt*. The Prophet ﷺ was with the Companions, yet he never criticized anyone's glorification of Allah or any kind of remembrance that conformed to the rulings of the Sharia.

This is the Prophetic guidance that we must follow in a balanced manner, avoiding extremes of laxity or harshness. It is essential to put everything in its proper place: to differentiate between what is forbidden, disliked, and permissible; between what is recommended and obligatory; and to distinguish between rulings of scholarly consensus and others where there are differences of opinion. The Sharia guides us on how to have moderation and balance in our dealings. Following a particular legal school (*madhhab*) should not lead to conflict or animosity; rather, it should foster tolerance and strengthen our connection to others. It should promote more understanding, refine our character, and be a means for goodness to spread.

We cannot deviate from sacred texts that are definitive in their authen-

140 Translator's note: they were repeating, *"Labbayk Allāhumma labbayk"* [Here I am, at Your service, O Allah! At Your service].

141 Narrated by Muslim in *Kitāb al-Ḥajj* (Hadith 1284).

ticity (*qaṭʿī al-thubūt*) and definitive in their meaning (*qaṭʿī al-dalāla*) regardless of the situation. Outside of these cases, there *is* room for different authoritative opinions. This principle helps us understand some of the Sharia's breadth, making us more open to those who follow other schools and opinions, so long as they do not create conflict or contradict a ruling on which there is consensus in Islam.

If we are open enough to engage and have a dialogue with non-Muslims, then surely there is ample room to collaborate with and benefit from other Muslims who share our fundamental belief in the foundation of all foundations: the testimony that there is no god but Allah and that Muhammad is the Messenger of Allah. This is what the Messenger of Allah ﷺ taught his Ummah. When we follow his teachings, harm is averted, the devil retreats, and the whisperings that influence many hearts and souls dissipate. Muslims are then able to work together and assist one another in spreading goodness.

One of the wise and righteous callers to Allah رحمه الله was asked why there was a separation between his group and another group, despite their being in the same town and following the same religion. He responded, "The difference between us is that we are located in this part of town, and they are located in another part of town." In other words, we are unified in our origin and goal. Someone then objected, "They are working hard to build mosques, but we don't see your group doing that!" He replied, "We need mosques to be built, and we need people to direct worshippers to pray in them. They build, and we send people to pray there. Therefore, we complement each other." His approach helps avoid evil whisperings that impact people's hearts and cause division between them.

We ask Allah to make us firm upon the correct way of understanding the Sharia and that He grants us etiquette with Him and with His servants for His sake—and success is by Allah alone. May Allah's peace and blessings be upon our master Muhammad, and upon his Family and Companions. All praise belongs to Allah, Lord of the Worlds.

CHAPTER 27

Attending to the Ending of Our Lives

All praise belongs to Allah, the Most Generous Sovereign. May Allah's peace and blessings be upon His Chosen Servant, the possessor of supreme virtue, and upon his Family, Companions, and whoever follows him along his Straight Path.

To proceed: Endings are extremely important. Being mindful of how we end our days, weeks, months, and years is valuable treasure of the Kingdom of the Heart. By being conscious of this, we hope that Allah ﷻ will grant us the favor of sealing our lives with goodness. As the Prophet ﷺ said, *"Actions are judged according to their endings."*[142]

HOW THE RIGHTEOUS SEEK A GOOD ENDING

The Ummah's sages, those endowed with intelligence, knowledge, and virtue, give great attention to the ending of their lives. They persistently ask Allah ﷻ for a good ending and weep profusely out of fear of a bad ending.

When we contemplate how people's hearts and states are constantly changing, we realize that we cannot dictate how our own lives will end

142 Narrated by al-Bukhārī in *Kitāb al-Riqāq* (Hadith 6128).

and only Allah can grace us with a good ending. In most cases, a person dies in the state which he lived, reflecting the convictions rooted in his heart and his direction in life. With that being said, there are exceptions. Allah ﷾ is the Turner of Hearts and He manifests unexpected outcomes continuously (guiding whomever He wills, even at the last moment; and allowing whomever He wills to go astray). This compels us to maintain humility and neediness before Him, always asking Him for a good ending.[143]

If one is blessed with attending to the end of his day and night, the end of his week and month, the end of his year, and the end of his Prayer, Quranic recitation, supplication, or any other action, he merits Allah favoring him with a good ending to life and beautifying his state when meeting Him ﷾.

Therefore, we must direct our concern to how we end our actions. A Hadith states, *"When a man retires to his bed, an angel and a devil hasten to him. The angel says, 'End with goodness,' and the devil says, 'End with evil.'"*[144] Whichever of the two he inclines towards, that one overtakes him. You either conclude your day and night's record with good, or you choose to conclude it with evil—and we seek refuge in Allah ﷾ from that.

Reflect on the conclusion of your day shortly before sunset. Observe Allah's ﷾ command to glorify Him by saying, *"Subḥān Allāh"* before sunset, and you will understand the essence of a good ending to the day. Look at how Allah ﷾ praises those who seek His forgiveness at the end of the night, and you will understand some of the significance of ending the night with goodness.

Try to end your Prayers in the best way. Have presence of heart and

143 Translator's note: the reality of one's ending (*khātima*) is from the unseen, teaching us not to pass ultimate judgment on others and to maintain awe and fear of Allah ﷾ when engaging in righteous actions to protect ourselves from self-admiration (*'ujb*). See al-Bukhārī (Hadith 3208) and Muslim (2643).

144 Narrated by al-Nasā'ī in *Kitāb 'Amal al-Yawm wa'l Layla.*

awareness throughout the entire Prayer and give special care to its end. Be the same when reciting the Quran and with all other righteous actions.

Ponder the passing of the months so that you end them with goodness. Reflect on how your Prophet ﷺ would exert extra effort at the end of Ramadan. Many heedless people might exert themselves at the beginning of the month, but at its end they spend their time in places of amusement or buying clothing in order to show off, in complete neglect of Islamic etiquette. On *Laylat al-Qadr*, some might engage in looking at forbidden things, speaking about evil matters, arguing with others, severing ties with relatives, or harming neighbors—missing out on immense good. This is the night about which the Messenger of Allah ﷺ said, *"Whoever is deprived of it is deprived of all goodness. Only a wretched person is deprived of its good."*[145]

We should diligently seek out *Laylat al-Qadr* and end the month of Ramadan specifically (and every other month generally) with sincere repentance and brokenness before Allah ﷻ, greater determination to establish Allah's commands, a desire for Allah's rewards, and an increased fear of Him. We should leave the month of Ramadan embodying the Messenger of Allah's teachings ﷺ both inwardly and outwardly.

When someone takes on more of the Prophet's character traits after Ramadan, this is a sign that his devotions in Ramadan have been accepted. This trains him to be steadfast in faith which results ultimately in him receiving a good ending. **"Allah makes the believers steadfast with the firm word ⌜of faith⌝ in this worldly life and in the Hereafter. And Allah leaves wrongdoers to stray. For Allah does what He wills."** [Quran 14:27]

145 Narrated by Ibn Māja in *Kitāb al-Ṣiyām* (Hadith 1644).

ETIQUETTES THAT ASSIST IN ATTAINING A GOOD ENDING

There are various practices that the Prophet ﷺ taught us to help someone who is at the end of his life. For example, when visiting a sick person who appears to be dying, increase his hope in Allah's mercy ﷻ, and recite Sūra Yā-Sīn when his soul seems close to departing. We should also repeat, *"Lā ilāha illā Allāh"* to the dying person, being careful not pressure or force him to say it, out of fear that the dying person becomes irritated and ends his life refusing to say it. If we hear him say, *"Lā ilāha illā Allāh"* or if he indicates that he affirms it, we should stop speaking unless he then says something else. This is so that his final words be, *"Lā ilāha illā Allāh."* Additionally, there should be no statues or the like in the house or a woman whose head is uncovered, as these prevent the angels of mercy from entering. These practices serve as essential measures to prepare the dying person for a good ending.

Everyone is exposed to trials at the time of the soul's departure. They are the devil's final attempts to misguide that person. Iblīs may appear in the form of a dead person whom the dying person had known. He tries to deceive him by saying, "I died before you and found that the best religion is Christianity," or ". . .is Judaism," or something else. He then will ask, "Do you believe in that religion?" The person might then say with his last breath, "Yes!" thereby dying outside of Islam. We seek refuge in Allah ﷻ, and we ask Him to protect us from an evil end!

ATTACHMENT TO SINS CAUSES AN EVIL ENDING

Much of a person's experiences when dying are the results of his deeds. What is especially perilous are the sins that he considered insignificant, which might even be the cause for a bad ending. Once, a man who was dying was unable to say *"Lā ilāha illā Allāh"* despite being able to say other things. Someone asked, "What's wrong with you?" He responded, "I am prevented from saying it because of a forbidden glance that I neither regretted nor repented from." That glance became a barrier between him and *"Lā ilāha illā Allāh"* at his time of death.

It is not necessary for a Muslim to say *"Lā ilāha illā Allāh"* at death for his belief in it is enough. Although if he is granted the enabling grace to say it, then his book of deeds concludes with a merit that allows him to enter Paradise without reckoning, as the Prophet ﷺ said, *"Whoever's last words are* 'Lā ilāha illā Allāh' *will enter Paradise."*[146] This means that he will enter with the foremost (*al-Sābiqūn*), which is an honor given to those whose lives end with this pure statement.

We must never be neglectful of this statement. We must recite it abundantly throughout our lives and contemplate its meanings. It allows us to realize the true meaning of Allah's Oneness and reach direct knowledge of Him ﷻ (*maʿrifa*). It is the best and most virtuous of statements and the greatest *dhikr*. Whenever a person says it in abundance with presence of heart, it produces light in the heart, inward purity, and washes away the evil of sins. A Hadith states, *"The most virtuous statement I and the Prophets before me said is:* Lā ilāha illā Allāh, waḥdahu lā sharīka lah, lahu'l mulk wa lahu'l ḥamd, yuḥyī wa yumīt wa Huwa Ḥayyun lā yamūt, biyadihi'l khayr, wa Huwa ʿalā kulli shayy'in Qadīr [There is no god but Allah, One without partner. To Him belongs the dominion and all praise is His. He gives life and death, and He is Living and does not die. All good is in His hand, and He has power over all things]."[147] We should repeat this *dhikr* out loud in marketplaces and shopping centers. The Prophet ﷺ told us that if someone enters the marketplace and recites it, *"Allah records one million good deeds for him, removes one million sins from him, and raises him one million degrees."*[148] These are the fortunes given to those who value the treasures of this religion.

146 Narrated by Abū Dawūd in *Kitāb al-Janāʾiz* (Hadith 3116) and by al-Ḥākim on the authority of Muʿādh, and he classified it as having an authentic chain of narration.

147 Narrated by Mālik in *al-Muwaṭṭaʾ* in *Kitāb al-Ḥajj* (Hadith 255).

148 Narrated by al-Tirmidhī in *Bāb al-Daʿawāt ʿan Rasūl Illāh* ﷺ (Hadith 3488) and al-Ḥākim in *al-Mustadrak* on the authority of ʿUmar ibn al-Khaṭṭāb.

Sometimes, a person who goes insane continues to repeat something that his heart was attached to. Likewise, during the throes of death, your heart is taken to what it was attached to during your life. For example, when a person who loved cars loses his mind, he might become obsessed with cars and even mimic their movement. Or when a person loses his mind who may have been very attached to the Prayer (or any other act of goodness), he then performs that action's movements over and over again. When you are overcome by the throes of death, you too will remember and return to whatever ruled your heart.

Being mindful of endings, such as the endings of months that pass us by, is one way we seek a good ending to our lives. Recognizing that we do not know how our lives will end protects us from vanity (*'ujb*) and from being impressed with our own good deeds. Having reverence for Allah's command ﷻ is one of the most powerful ways to seek a good ending. On the other hand, harming others, failing to give people their rights, and making false claims about one's spiritual rank and level of knowledge are some of the most dangerous causes for a bad ending.

Choose your words carefully as they might be your last. Take the utmost benefit from the life that you have. Beware of the devil's plot to delude you and cause you to become proud of yourself and thus neglect how you end your life. Allah ﷻ kept this matter hidden so that we maintain proper etiquette with Him and remain in awe of Him until we meet Him. When we do so, He will grant us safety and His everlasting contentment.

O Allah, we ask You for the enabling grace (*tawfiq*) to do that which You love and for You to grant us a good ending. O Allah, make good our ultimate end and the endings of all our affairs, and protect us from disgrace in this world and the punishment of the Hereafter. May Allah's peace and blessings be upon our master Muhammad, his Family, and his Companions. All praise belongs to Allah, Lord of the Worlds.

CHAPTER 28

Refraining from Sin

All praise belongs to Allah, the Merciful Sovereign, the Vigilant Reckoner, the Most Generous Giver of Blessings who encompasses all things in His Knowledge and takes account of everything. He sent His Prophet Muhammad to us with guidance and the religion of truth. Through him, every sound heart finds guidance and feet are made firm on the Straight Path. O Allah, send blessings and peace upon our master Muhammad, his Family and Companions, and upon those beloved and near to him.

To proceed: In the Kingdom of the Heart that Allah has bestowed upon us, it is necessary to understand the following reality: that refraining from forbidden things is the sign of being genuine in worship, the realization of faith, and the means for attaining Allah's good pleasure ﷻ. Refraining from forbidden things is one of the distinguishing traits of the sincere and penitent.

Some of the pious predecessors were deliberating on what the greatest act of righteousness was. Each scholar suggested a different type of worship until one of them said, "The best act of worship is abandoning sins." The rest said, "That's it! That's it! The best act of obedience is abandoning sins."

SAFEGUARDING THE TONGUE & PRIVATES

Our heart and limbs are exposed to various forbidden acts that we must refrain from. Allah ﷻ forbade arrogance, vanity, ostentation, deception, envy, hatred, and other sins of the heart. Allah ﷻ also made certain actions pertaining to each limb forbidden, two of which require special regulation. When the Prophet Muhammad ﷺ was asked about what causes most people to enter the Fire, he said, *"The two hollow areas: the mouth and the private parts."*[149] By diligently regulating these two limbs, we become truly devout, felicitous, and attain rewards beyond our imagination.

These two areas are unique due to their powerful and extensive impact when used in ways that are forbidden by Allah ﷻ, leading to damnation and punishment. A believer must observe the strength of his faith, which grows through proper restraint of the tongue and private parts. Regulating the mouth extends beyond speech to include food consumption as well.

Allah ﷻ mentions the traits of His believing servants who inherit the Garden of Firdaws. He says ﷻ, **"Those who guard their chastity, except with their wives or those ⌜bondswomen⌝ in their possession, for then they are free from blame, but whoever seeks beyond that, they are the transgressors."** [Quran 23:5–7] Those who go beyond the limits of human dignity, the Sacred Law, and etiquette with their Creator are called transgressors.

The Sharia aims to refine the individual and elevate him so that he does not give in to fleeting pleasures. These are beneath his noble station and immense value with Allah ﷻ, and they endanger his ultimate end everlasting kingdom of unending blessings. The devil's forces and the enemies of human dignity unite to urge people to fulfill forbidden

149 Narrated by Aḥmad and al-Ḥākim, who said its chain of transmission is authentic, on the authority of Abū Hurayra.

desires, serving neither society nor humanity, but rather waging war with human dignity and honor.

EXCELLENCE IN REFRAINING FROM SIN

Refraining from sin is the distinguishing quality of the pious. Engaging in various acts of worship alone (such fasting Ramadan, Prayer, recitation of the Quran, etc.) are not enough if one is not steadfast in refraining from forbidden things. Just as we are encouraged to perform good deeds with excellence, an emphasis is also placed on excellence in refraining from forbidden things.

Safeguarding the private parts is crucial, since protecting them from sin is a means for being saved from abasement. Allah ﷻ abases those who uninhibitedly act on their desires and prefer immediate pleasures over what the Lord of the heavens and earth commands. From the moment these people are resurrected, they are tied to their private parts, their faces aflame in shame before all, then they are suspended in the Fire, with pus seeping from their private parts—along with other punishments that have been narrated by the Prophet ﷺ, who Allah ﷻ entrusted with conveying the message on His behalf.[150]

PROHIBITING THE PRECURSORS OF SIN

To refrain from forbidden actions, we must refrain from their precursors. Three stages precede the sins of the private parts: looking, thinking, and talking. Once one engages in the first stage, it becomes difficult to prevent the following stages. The Prophet ﷺ stated that the eye, tongue, and heart have their own forms of fornication.[151] By shielding oneself

150 Narrated by Imam Muhammad ibn Aḥmad al-Dhahabī in *al-Kabāʾir.*

151 This is an indication of the Hadith narrated by Aḥmad on the authority of Abū Hurayra, *"The eye fornicates, and the heart fornicates. The eye's fornication is a gaze, and the heart's fornication is longing."*

from the evil of these precursors, the private parts will be safeguarded from committing an enormity.

The first stage is looking. The gaze impacts the heart, sowing the seeds of desire and temptation. The gaze is explicitly identified in the Quran, among all other actions, because it initiates this act. It is then followed by unrestrained thoughts that stir the desire to act. Allah ﷻ said, "⌜**O Prophet**⌝**, tell the believing men to lower their gaze and guard their private parts. That is purer for them. Surely, Allah is All-Aware of what they do. And tell the believing women to lower their gaze and guard their private parts, and not to reveal their adornments except what normally appears. Let them draw their veils over their chests. . .**" [Quran 24:30–31] to the end of the verse. The Prophet ﷺ said, *"A forbidden glance is a poisoned arrow from the quiver of Iblīs. Allah says, '**Whoever resists it out of fear of Me, I replace it with a faith, the sweetness of which he finds in his heart.**'"*[152] One who lowers his gaze receives a reward and experiences its impact immediately. Additionally, a greater and more generous reward is in store for him in the Hereafter.

Looking at people's property, whether it be their houses, gardens, or cars is permissible. Allah ﷻ did not command us to lower our gaze from these things, unlike other things that stir lustful desires. Having a desire to attain these types of wealth is permissible, though extending one's hand to wrongfully take it is forbidden. On the other hand, with carnal desires, it is difficult to separate the three stages from each other. Divine commands were revealed to protect, refine, and elevate humanity by making the lustful gaze forbidden and closing the door at the very onset.

The second stage is our thoughts. We must elevate our thinking because our thoughts have a substantial impact on our desires. With regards to desirous thoughts, Allah ﷻ has said, "**Whether you reveal what is in your hearts or conceal it, Allah will call you to account for**

152 Narrated by al-Ḥākim which he classified as authentic on the authority of Ḥudhayfa, and by al-Ṭabarānī on the authority of Ibn Mas'ūd.

it. He forgives whomever He wills and punishes whomever He wills. And Allah is Most Capable of everything." [Quran 2:284] Whenever a passing thought comes, we must ward it off with the remembrance of Allah ﷻ. We must reflect on the ultimate end, of standing before the Judge Who has power over us, is more aware of us, and encompasses all things in His knowledge ﷻ. What will be your state if He asks you, "Why did you turn your head? Why did you look?" And how will you be when you are asked about even more serious sins?

The third stage is talking about those forbidden desires. This is the fornication of speech that the Prophet ﷺ informed us of in the Hadith, *"The fornication of the tongue is speech."*[153] When a person sincerely guards his eyes from looking, his tongue from speaking, his heart from thinking about the desire, and his stomach from excessive satiation, there is a greater probability that he will be protected from falling into sin. Such a person will be safe from the many traps set by those who desire to sow corruption on the earth.

Allah ﷻ said, **"It is Allah's will to make things clear to you, guide you to the ⌜noble⌝ ways of those before you, and turn to you in mercy. For Allah is All-Knowing, All-Wise. And it is Allah's will to turn to you ⌜in grace⌝, but those who follow their desires wish to see you deviate entirely."** [Quran 4:26- 27] In these verses, Allah ﷻ clarifies the attempts that people make to seduce others and lead them into sin. These teachings open our inner sight so that we take what benefits us and forsake what harms us, and by doing so, become people of piety. When the Messenger of Allah ﷺ was asked about what enters most people into Paradise, he said, *"Mindfulness of Allah* (taqwā) *and beautiful character."*[154]

O Allah, grant us the reality of *taqwā* and beautiful character. Protect

153 Narrated by al-Bukhārī in *Kitāb al-Istiʾdhān* (Hadith 5889) and Muslim in *Kitāb al-Qadar* (Hadith 2675).

154 Narrated by Aḥmad and al-Ḥākim, who classified its chain of transmission as authentic, on the authority of Abū Hurayra.

us from vile actions, both the outward and the inward, and make us of those who are true. Protect us from being exposed to punishment and tribulation—O Lord of the Worlds! May Allah's peace and blessings be upon our master Muhammad, and upon his Family and Companions. All praise belongs to Allah, Lord of the Worlds.

CHAPTER 29

The Impact of Intention & Firm Resolve

All praise belongs to Allah, the Most Generous Sovereign, the Exalted, the Most Merciful. We bear witness that He is Allah, there is no god except Him, One without partner. And we bear witness that our Prophet, our master Muhammad, is His Servant and Messenger. He sent him with guidance and the religion of truth to make it prevail over all other religions to the dismay of the polytheists.

To proceed: A key factor in the governance of the Kingdom of the Heart is one's aim and intention. By rectifying our aim and resolve, we achieve significant outcomes and benefits in this life and in the Hereafter. Likewise, evil intentions and the resolve to engage in disobedience have terrible consequences, exposing people to different types of harm and to Allah's wrath ﷻ and punishment in the Fire.

One of the signs of the soundness and acceptance of our devotional acts is that after completing the action, a genuine resolve to perform other acts of obedience arises within our hearts. We then engage in actions that bring benefit to us and others and are full of rewards. Simultaneously, we wholeheartedly shun all sins and acts of disobedience. One of the righteous from the first generations of the Ummah, emphasizing the profound impact of intentions, said, "Whoever initiates for himself a good intention, Allah opens seventy doors of enabling grace (*tawfiq*) for him. And whoever initiates for himself an evil intention, Allah opens seventy doors from the doors of abasement for him." We seek refuge in Allah ﷻ.

When a person decides wholeheartedly to do something, many amazing things take place due to the strength of his resolve. But if his goals are lowly and his intentions are malicious, he abases himself and darkness quickly envelops him. He finds himself engaging in acts of disobedience which cut him off from his Lord. This is the significant impact that intention and resolve have on our spiritual states.

COMPONENTS OF A GOOD INTENTION & STRONG RESOLVE

When achieving one's goal, a believer must cultivate good intentions, a strong resolve, and true orientation to Allah. In the various actions, supplications, and recitations that we have been taught, we have been given the means to ask for firm resolve. In every Prayer we turn to Allah ﷻ saying, **"Guide us along the Straight Path, the Path of those You have blessed—not those who have incurred anger, nor those who have gone astray."** [Quran 1:6–7] If we make this supplication with presence of heart, we will become determined to resemble those whom Allah ﷻ has blessed from among the Prophets, the Entirely True (*Ṣiddiqūn*), the martyrs, and the righteous. It instills in us a desire to emulate their example, resemble them, and embody their noble qualities and states.

This supplication also makes us aware of the evil of the disbelievers who have incurred Allah's anger and went astray. We differentiate ourselves from them by aligning our character, orientation, and intention with the Sharia and divine guidance. This elevated approach raises us above the abasement others experience by following their desires, preferring immediate pleasures, and neglecting noble virtues. In all these aspects, the believer learns to rectify his resolve and intention before he embarks on any endeavor. When commenting on the meaning of the

Hadith, *"Actions are judged according to intentions, and to each person is what he intended. . ."* Ibn Raslān al-Shāfiʿī said, "You must rectify your intention before engaging in the action."

EXPANDING THE INTENTION & MAKING IT SINCERELY FOR ALLAH ﷻ

The Prophet ﷺ said, *"A believer's intention is better than his action."* This is because a genuine intention is not tainted by ostentation or vanity, whereas the action is subject to those defects, which could deprive an individual of its reward. This is one aspect of the Hadith.

The second aspect is that whenever the intention is sound, Allah ﷻ compensates it with an immense and great reward that far exceeds the reward that the act itself merited.

A third meaning is that a believer's intention can greatly surpass the actual action. He might aspire to achieve something that is currently beyond his capacity, hoping to do it if the opportunity ever arises. Thus, despite the excellence of his actions—such as charity, fulfilling promises, being a good neighbor, maintaining family ties, assisting those in difficulty—all these actions still fall short of what he intends. He intends and resolves to do more, and to perform even greater and more virtuous deeds. While doing what is within his ability, his intention still goes beyond that. In all that he does, he seeks Allah's good pleasure ﷻ, hastens to do good, and aims to attain great rewards.

The hypocrite, on the other hand, may outwardly engage in a virtuous act, yet his intention is evil. He does not love to perform the action and lacks any praiseworthy intention.

The believer must then be aware of his orientation and resolve. He must strengthen and expand the sphere of his intention, purifying it of blemishes, and making it solely for Allah's sake ﷻ. If he does this, he will see the signs that his actions are accepted. If, for example, he ends

Ramadan with a greater dedication to strengthening and expanding his intentions, then this is a sign that his devotions during that month have been accepted. The enabling grace he has been granted, which is to remain steadfast, is a blessing from Allah that is a means for celebration—and what a celebration! And by continuing to remain steadfast in obeying Allah's commands سبحانه وتعالى, the believer prepares himself for an endless Eid celebration.

This was 'Alī ibn Abī Ṭālib's response رضي الله عنه when someone gave him the Eid greeting: "Today is Eid, yesterday was Eid, and tomorrow, *in shā' Allāh*, will be Eid. Each day in which we do not disobey Allah is Eid." On such a day we receive a greater portion of Allah's blessings and gain closeness to Him سبحانه وتعالى. We achieve this through having genuine resolve, which opens the doors of enabling grace and instantly brings us mercy.

Do not miss the opportunity to expand and strengthen your intention when performing righteous actions. To the best of your ability, specify and elaborate on the intentions of your endeavors that relate to yourself, your family and children, your community, your colleagues, and those you engage with in different situations. By doing so, you attain one of the treasures of divine favor by way of your intention and by being sincere in seeking Allah's Countenance سبحانه وتعالى. This treasure is a garment that adorns and honors the believer. It is not removed from him at death but remains with him until the Appointed Day. As for other garments, no matter how lavish they are, they will eventually be removed. As our Lord سبحانه وتعالى said, **"The clothing of righteousness—that is best."** [Quran 7:26]

THE BLESSINGS OF ACTIONS ARE IN INTENTIONS

Allah سبحانه وتعالى has opened the doors of intention for us, allowing us to make numerous righteous intentions for one righteous action, thereby multiplying its reward. It has been said, "The actions of the Entirely True (*Ṣiddīqūn*) became pure by way of their intentions." This is due to the expansiveness and abundance of their intentions. When entering or leaving the home, they have righteous intentions regarding whom they meet along the way, intending to initiate the greeting of *salām* and be the first to extend their hand, which removes resentment from people's hearts.

The righteous also have expansive intentions in their recitation of the Quran, such as deriving noble types of knowledge, seeking the downpour of Allah's immense mercy ﷾, and removing impurities from their hearts. They also intend to plunge deep into its meanings and wonders, seeking to comprehend the secrets of its commands, hoping that the word of Allah becomes infused with their hearts and bodies.

When reciting Quran in a group, we can include the intentions of allowing others to hear, exposing ourselves and others to Allah's mercy by embracing the meanings deeply within all of our hearts, and enhancing the understanding of all those present. Additional intentions include seeking to be mentioned in the Highest Realm (as promised by Allah ﷾), to be immersed in His mercy, to have serenity descend upon us, to be surrounded by the angels, to have our hearts become gentler and purer, and to attain nearness to the Most High ﷾.

Intentions do not just apply to acts of worship. Our intentions transform merely permissible actions into acts of obedience. We must therefore elevate our day-to-day habits and actions through the intentions we make. Conversely, corrupt intentions damage acts of obedience. As a result, a person loses the reward and could even be punished. Good intentions do not impact forbidden acts whatsoever, just as something that is inherently impure cannot be purified by washing it. Doing something that Allah ﷾ has forbidden with a good intention will not change that action.

This helps us recognize the significant opportunity we have been given when it comes to beautifying our intentions. Let us not waste this opportunity. Welcome each day and night with righteous intentions and a genuine resolve to be upright, to perform acts of goodness, and to be distant from evil. Then we will be granted enabling grace, assistance, and success.

O Allah, You are the One who granted good people the enabling grace to perform good and assisted them in doing so, so grant us Your enabling grace to perform good and assist us in doing so—by Your mercy, O Most Merciful! May Allah's peace and blessings be upon our master Muhammad, and upon his Family and Companions. All praise belongs to Allah, Lord of the Worlds.

CHAPTER 30

The Meaning of Eid

All praise belongs to Allah, a praise that uplifts the hearts. May Allah's peace and blessings be upon His Chosen Servant, the guide, our master Muhammad, the most upright and grateful, and upon his Family and Companions, and upon the possessors of cultivated hearts who follow them with excellence.

To proceed: The great Kingdom of the Heart impacts believers whose entire beings have become colored by Allah's religion. This gives them deep and subtle understandings of the meaning of Eid as it relates to receiving benefit and assistance from Allah ﷻ. **"This is Allah's ˹way˺ of coloring—and who gives a better color than Allah? And we worship ˹none but˺ Him."** [Quran 2:138] We alluded to this understanding previously when quoting the statement of 'Alī ibn Abū Ṭālib ﵁, "Each day in which we do not disobey Allah is Eid."

We consider Eid and its connection to the ultimate return to Allah ﷻ from this perspective. The two primary days of Eid are Eid al-Fiṭr and Eid al-Aḍḥā, which have been given a unique status and distinction. One of these distinctions is the Sunna of proclaiming Allah's greatness (*takbīr*) on the night preceding both Eids, and proclaiming the *takbīr* after the Prayers for Eid al-Aḍḥā specifically.[155] Allah ﷻ said, **"So that you may**

155 Translator's note: Saying, *"Allāhu Akbar"* [Allah is truly Great].

complete the prescribed period," meaning the month of Ramadan, **"and proclaim the greatness of Allah in having guided you."** [Quran 2:185] The *takbīr* was designated as the expression for Eid so that we increase in reverence for Allah the Truly Great, the Most High ﷻ. The *takbīr* lifts the veils that prevent us from revering Allah and realizing the exaltedness of our connection to Him. It also motivates us to fully prepare for the meeting with and return to Him ﷻ.

THE MEANING OF EID

Another important aspect of Eid is the Eid Prayer that is recommended on both Eid al-Fiṭr and Eid al-Aḍḥā. Some of the scholars of *Tafsīr* mention that both Eids are alluded to in the Quran. Allah ﷻ says, **"Successful indeed is the one who purifies himself, remembers the Name of his Lord, and prays."** [Quran 87:14–15]

In one opinion, **"Successful indeed is the one who purifies himself,"** refers to *Zakāt al-Fiṭr*, which is paid at the end of Ramadan; **"remembers the Name of his Lord,"** refers to proclaiming Allah's greatness (*takbīr*); **"and prays"** refers to the Eid Prayer. Another opinion holds that Allah's words ﷻ, **"So pray to your Lord and sacrifice"** [Quran 108:2] refer to the Eid al-Aḍḥā Prayer followed by sacrificing animals.

We mentioned previously the statement of Jesus the son of Maryam ﵇, **"O Allah, our Lord! Send us a table spread from heaven, which will be a celebration for us—the first and last of us."** [Quran 5:114] This illustrates that when Eid arrives, it evokes emotions and connects us to events that took place in our sacred history. A wise man once said, "Eid is not merely for the one who wears new clothing; rather, the true Eid is for the one whose acts of obedience increase. Eid is not for he whose appearance impresses others; rather, the true Eid is for he whose sins are forgiven."

Through this understanding of Eid, you realize that a believer has much cause to celebrate the gifts and support he receives from his Lord ﷻ. He experiences continuous joy from the successive outpouring of Allah's favors upon him. A believer receives these favors through righteous actions, spending in charity, and by taking advantage of the time that he has been given.

Through these actions, a believer prepares for a greater Eid: the day he meets Allah ﷻ and Allah is well pleased with him and gives him the good news of His mercy, good pleasure, and gardens of everlasting bliss. This occurs when the believer has a good ending at death, loves to meet Allah, and Allah ﷻ loves to meet him. This is a greater Eid, and an immense and all-encompassing gift from Allah ﷻ. This understanding of Eid combines all of what is properly considered joyous through the lens of faith, which does not focus on beautifying and ornamenting the outward, but on realizing what is required to attain Allah's good pleasure and actualizing one's connection to Him ﷻ. It is through this that we attain felicity in this world, in the grave, and on the Day of Gathering, and we accompany those whom Allah has brought close to Him.

EID IN THE NEXT LIFE

If a person is given the honor of a good ending, then after death he experiences successive, never-ending Eids. His soul is welcomed with serenity and a sweet fragrance. When people carry his body to the grave, he calls out, "Take me ahead! Take me ahead to Paradise, divine contentment, and a Lord who is not displeased!"

It is completely different, however, for the one who does not have a good ending and does not meet his Lord with firm faith. He calls out at his funeral procession, "Woe to me! Where is this funeral procession going?"[156]

156 Referring to the Hadith narrated by al-Bukhārī in his *Ṣaḥīḥ* on the authority of Abū Saʿīd al-Khudrī رضي الله عنه who said that the Prophet ﷺ used to say, *"When the funeral*

After this, the one who is granted a good end will be granted steadfastness when questioned in the grave, as mentioned in the noble Hadith, when the Prophet ﷺ received revelation of what people experience in the graves. Allah ﷻ says, **"Allah makes the believers steadfast with the firm word ˹of faith˺ in this worldly life and the Hereafter."** [Quran 14:27]

On the Day of Resurrection, which group will a person be with? If he is with the righteous who are safe from Allah's punishment, he experiences Eid. When he stands under the shade of the Banner of Praise, he experiences Eid. When the Scale of good deeds weighs heavier, he experiences Eid. When he receives his book of deeds in his right hand, he experiences Eid. When his deeds are presented and he receives beautiful benevolence and gentleness from Allah ﷻ, he experiences Eid. And after that, what a great Eid he experiences when it is announced, "So-and-so, son of so-and-so, has attained a felicity after which there is no damnation ever!" When his feet are steadfast as he crosses the Traverse and he passes over it with speed, he experiences Eid. When he sees Paradise and what Allah ﷻ has in store for him, the likes of which no eye has ever seen, no ear has ever heard, and no heart could ever imagine, he experiences Eid. When he enters Paradise behind the Chosen One ﷺ, he experiences Eid. He ﷺ is the one who said, *"I am the first to grasp Paradise's doorknocker, and Allah will then open it for me. He will then allow me to enter it, and with me are the believers who were poor. This is no boast."*[157]

After entering Paradise, its inhabitants will be granted further gifts from Allah ﷻ, **"There they will have whatever they desire, and with Us is ˹even˺ more."** [Quran 50:35] The various types of blessings in Paradise cannot be enumerated and its people continue to receive even more from Allah ﷻ. At every moment, the inhabitants of Paradise receive things

procession is prepared and the men carry the casket on their shoulders, if the deceased was righteous, he says, 'Take me ahead!' But if he was not righteous, he says to the procession, 'Woe to me! Where is this funeral procession going?' All things hear his voice except for people—and if people were to hear it, they would collapse."

157 Narrated by al-Tirmidhī in *al-Manāqib ʿan Rasūl Allāh* ﷺ (Hadith 3695).

that they never could imagine. Beyond all this is the greatest gift of gazing upon Allah's Noble Countenance ﷻ and receiving the fullest measure from His Presence ﷻ. All of these are Eids, and what Eids they are!

However, other people merely commemorate certain life events. Their celebrations are limited to these. They may express joy in their words or actions, but none of it has any permanence. When they die, they will have forgotten these moments. There is a big difference between their celebrations and the celebrations of the people of faith. We should appreciate the light, guidance, and dignity that our religion gives us. Those who are not true in faith and are not connected to the All-Merciful ﷻ have no portion of these blessings.

OUR PERCEPTION ELEVATES US

Only those who affirm Allah's Oneness ﷻ, who are near to Him, and who follow the path of guidance of the Prophet Muhammad ﷺ have this perception of Eid. Their hearts are full of yearning to meet Allah ﷻ and to see our master Muhammad ibn ʿAbd-Allah in the Barzakh, in Paradise, and on the Day of Gathering. They long to be shaded under his Banner of Praise and to drink from his Basin. These forms of spiritual yearning are distinctions given to the people of lofty ranks whose seek the priceless treasures of faith.

These are sacred, pure, and elevated yearnings by which Allah ﷻ distinguishes whomever He wills from His servants. Through these types of love, we hope to be like the great Companion Bilāl ؓ at his time of passing. When his wife sensed that death was imminent, she said, "What a calamity!" He then opened his eyes as he was experiencing the pangs of death and said to her, "Rather, what a joy this is! Tomorrow we will meet the beloved ones: Muhammad and his folk." How wondrous then is this yearning that elevates a person's state and gives him a true understanding of life, death, and what comes after.

We need to broaden our understanding of the concept of Eid, which is connected to our return to Allah ﷻ. When we do so, we place ourselves in a position to receive gifts from the Most Generous Sovereign. This understanding makes us hasten to perform actions that purify our hearts and guarantee us felicity on the Day of Resurrection.

We ask Allah ﷻ to make our days and nights Eids, celebrations of experiencing His closeness and contentment. We ask that He increases our good deeds and pardons our sins and misdeeds. We ask Allah ﷻ for the Eid of the good ending of dying upon Islam, followed by the Eid of meeting Him while He is pleased with us.

O believer: how wondrous is the Kingdom of the Heart that you have been given! When you realize the greatness of this blessing, it is only fitting that you do your utmost to perfect your dealings with Allah. You may then receive the most excellent reward by the Lord of Creation and He ﷻ will enter you into Paradise with those whom He loves.

We ask Allah to enter us into Paradise without reckoning. O Allah, make us steadfast, grant us uprightness, adorn us with nobility, grant us Your good pleasure, and treat us in a way befitting of You—O Most Generous, Most Giving! May Allah's peace and blessings be upon our master Muhammad, the Chosen One, and upon his Family and Companions. All praise belongs to Allah, Lord of the Worlds.

HABIB ʿUMAR IBN MUḤAMMAD IBN SĀLIM IBN ḤAFĪẒ IBN AL-SHAYKH ABŪ BAKR IBN SĀLIM

Habib ʿUmar ibn Muḥammad ibn Sālim ibn Ḥafīẓ is a direct descendent of the Prophet Muhammad ﷺ through his grandson Imam al-Ḥusayn. He was born in the blessed city of Tarīm, in the valley of Ḥaḍramawt in Yemen on the 4th of Muḥarram, 1383 H. which coincides with the 27th of May, 1963 C.E. He memorized the Quran as a child and was raised in a righteous household where his parents instilled within him knowledge, faith, and Prophetic character.

He first began seeking knowledge at the hands of the Mufti of Tarīm, his noble father, the great martyr, Habib Muhammad ibn Sālim ibn Ḥafīẓ. He also studied under the great scholars of Tarīm such as Habib Muḥammad ibn ʿAlawī ibn Shihāb al-Dīn, Habib Aḥmad ibn ʿAlī ibn al-Shaykh Abū Bakr, and Habib ʿAbd-Allāh ibn Shaykh al-ʿAydarūs. He also spent time studying in Al-Bayḍāʾ with Habib Muḥammad ibn ʿAbd-Allāh al-Haddār, as well as in the Two Holy Cities of Mecca and Madina, receiving the highest authorization from luminaries of the time, such as Habib Aḥmad Mashhūr al-Ḥaddād and Habib ʿAbd al-Qādir bin Aḥmad al-Saqqāf.

He is the Dean of Dār al-Muṣṭafā for the study of Islamic sciences in Tarim, which he founded in the year 1414 H./1994 C.E. He continues to travel globally to call people to Allah and revive the Prophetic way of knowledge and spiritual cultivation.